STEVEN HOLL: MAKING ARCHITECTURE

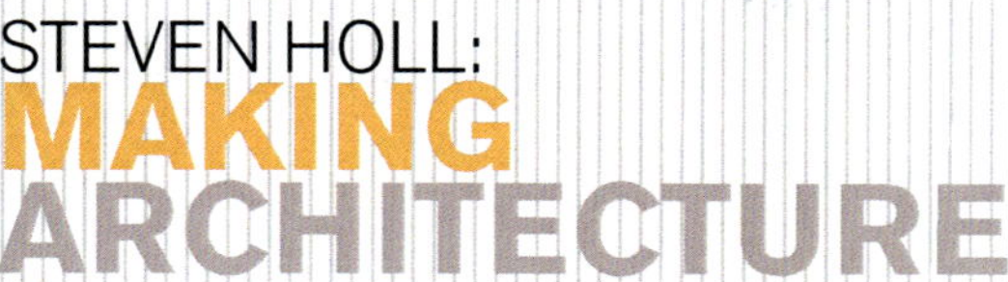

SAMUEL DORSKY MUSEUM OF ART
STATE UNIVERSITY OF NEW YORK AT NEW PALTZ

STEVEN HOLL:
MAKING ARCHITECTURE

CONTENTS

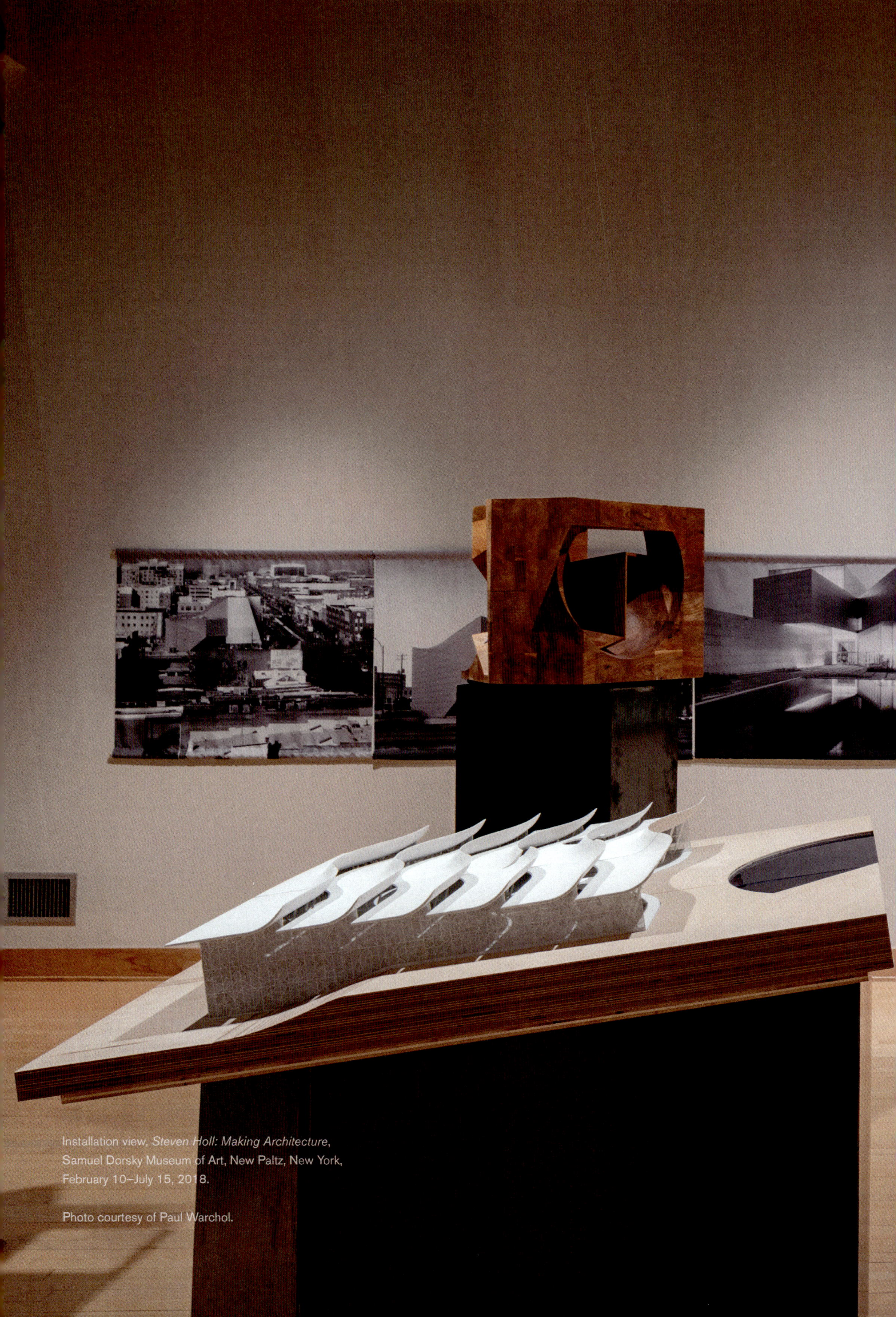

Installation view, *Steven Holl: Making Architecture*, Samuel Dorsky Museum of Art, New Paltz, New York, February 10–July 15, 2018.

Photo courtesy of Paul Warchol.

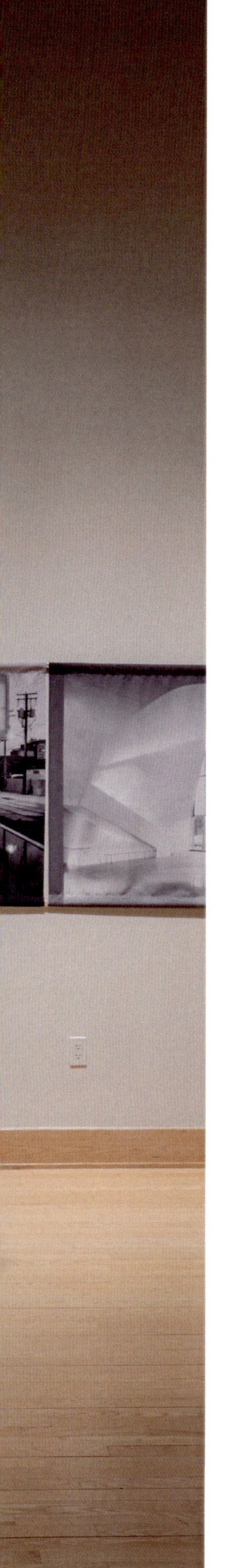

INTRODUCTION & DIRECTOR'S ACKNOWLEDGMENTS

The Dorsky Museum is pleased to present *Steven Holl: Making Architecture*, an exhibition and accompanying catalogue featuring work by one of the foremost architects in the world who also happens to be a long-time resident of the Hudson Valley.

A signature program of the museum, The Dorsky's "Hudson Valley Masters" series honors an artist whose work has made a significant contribution to the field of contemporary art and design. Artists are honored with one-person exhibitions that provide a survey of their careers and current work. The scholarly catalogues that accompany the exhibitions become part of a permanent archive documenting the region's rich contemporary art scene. Past Hudson Valley Masters have included Robert Morris, Lesley Dill, Don Nice, Judy Pfaff, Carolee Schneemann, and Dick Polich. Working in a variety of media, each of these masters has maintained a national and international career while living in the Hudson Valley region.

In 2018 we honor Steven Holl, a master architect, master watercolorist, and the creator of 'T' Space, a Hudson Valley gallery that presents interdisciplinary summer programs of music, poetry, architecture, and art in Rhinebeck, New York. Situated in the woods adjacent to Round Lake, 'T' Space provides a natural setting for the synthesis of multiple art forms and the presentation of original works of art that inspire artists and audiences alike. Like many artists who have lived and worked in the Hudson Valley, Holl has been influenced by the landscape and by the unique quality of the region's water and light. His watercolors, his sculptures, and his architecture (which can also be read as sculpture) find a way to capture this light as they reflect and incorporate the surrounding landscape.

I am immensely grateful to exhibition curator Nina Stritzler-Levine for her organization of this exhibition and for her excellent essay. The two additional essays within these pages are equally eloquent and thought provoking. Kerry Carso presents Holl's work in the context of the Hudson Valley architects who came before him who

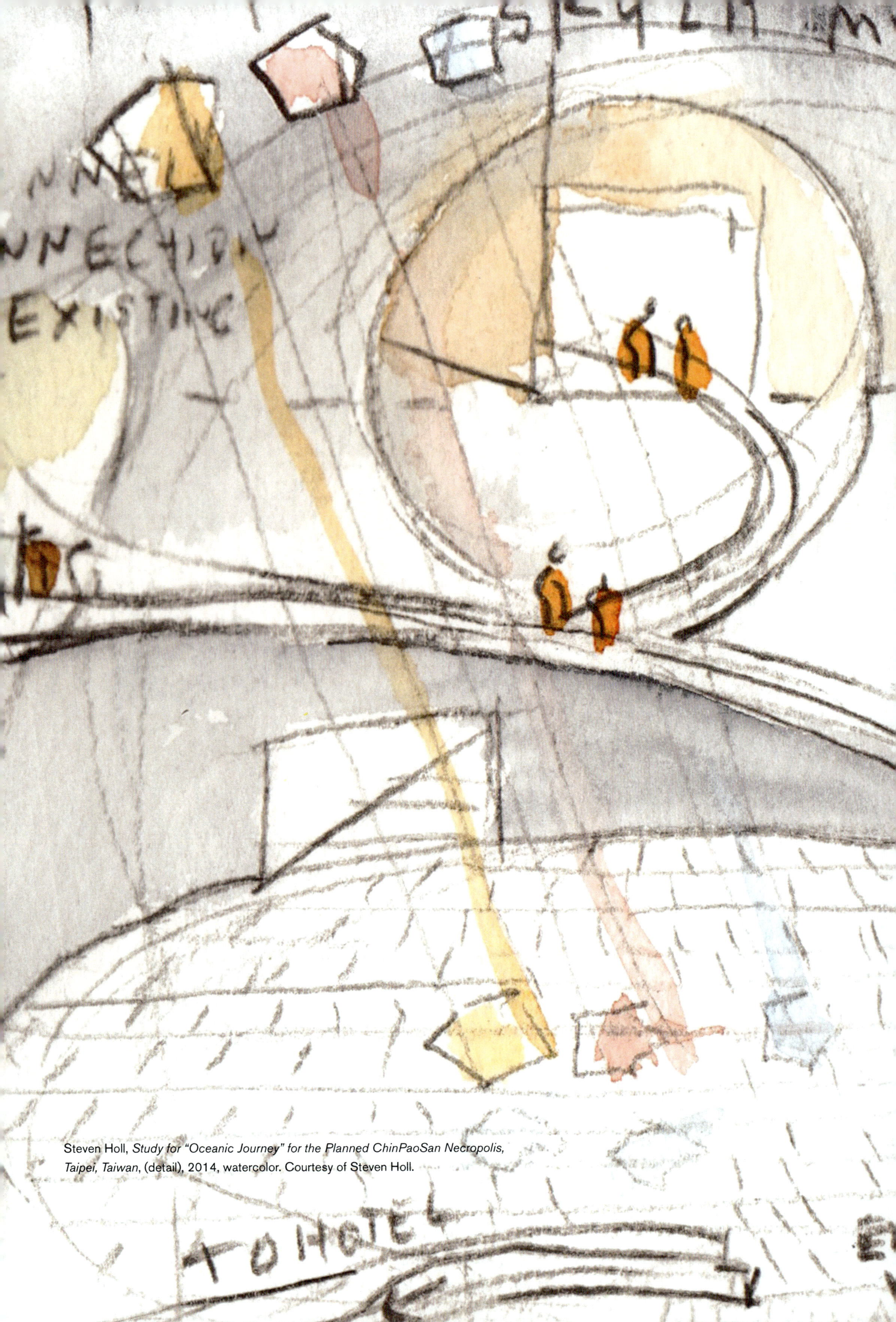

Steven Holl, *Study for "Oceanic Journey" for the Planned ChinPaoSan Necropolis, Taipei, Taiwan*, (detail), 2014, watercolor. Courtesy of Steven Holl.

also sought to create structures that were anchored in the land. Peter Olshavsky examines the relationship between architecture and phenomenology and Holl's understanding of the impact of architecture on the human body—how "architecture makes us what we are."

I am also grateful to SUNY New Paltz Senior Designer Jeff Lesperance for his inspired catalog design; Dorsky Museum Curator of Exhibitions and Programs Anastasia James for her excellent shepherding of catalogue as well as other printed materials related to the exhibition; catalogue editor Kristin Swan; and Dorsky Museum staff members Janis Benincasa, Zachary Bowman, Wayne Lempka, Amy Pickering, Bob Wagner, and Graduate Assistant Emily Brownawell for their contributions to the exhibition and related programs.

Special thanks go to the State University of New York at New Paltz and to the Friends of the Samuel Dorsky Museum of Art, both of which provide ongoing support for the museum's exhibitions and programs. Thank you also to SUNY New Paltz President Donald Christian and Provost Lorin Basden Arnold for their support of this and other exhibitions presented by The Dorsky Museum.

Last but certainly not least, I extend my heartfelt gratitude to Steven Holl and Dimitra Tsachrelia, as well as Jacobo Mingorance Arranz and Raechel Root of the Steven Myron Holl Foundation for their assistance in the development of this catalogue and exhibition. Their eager embrace of this project and the efforts that they have exerted to bring it to fruition are truly appreciated.

Sara J. Pasti
The Neil C. Trager Director

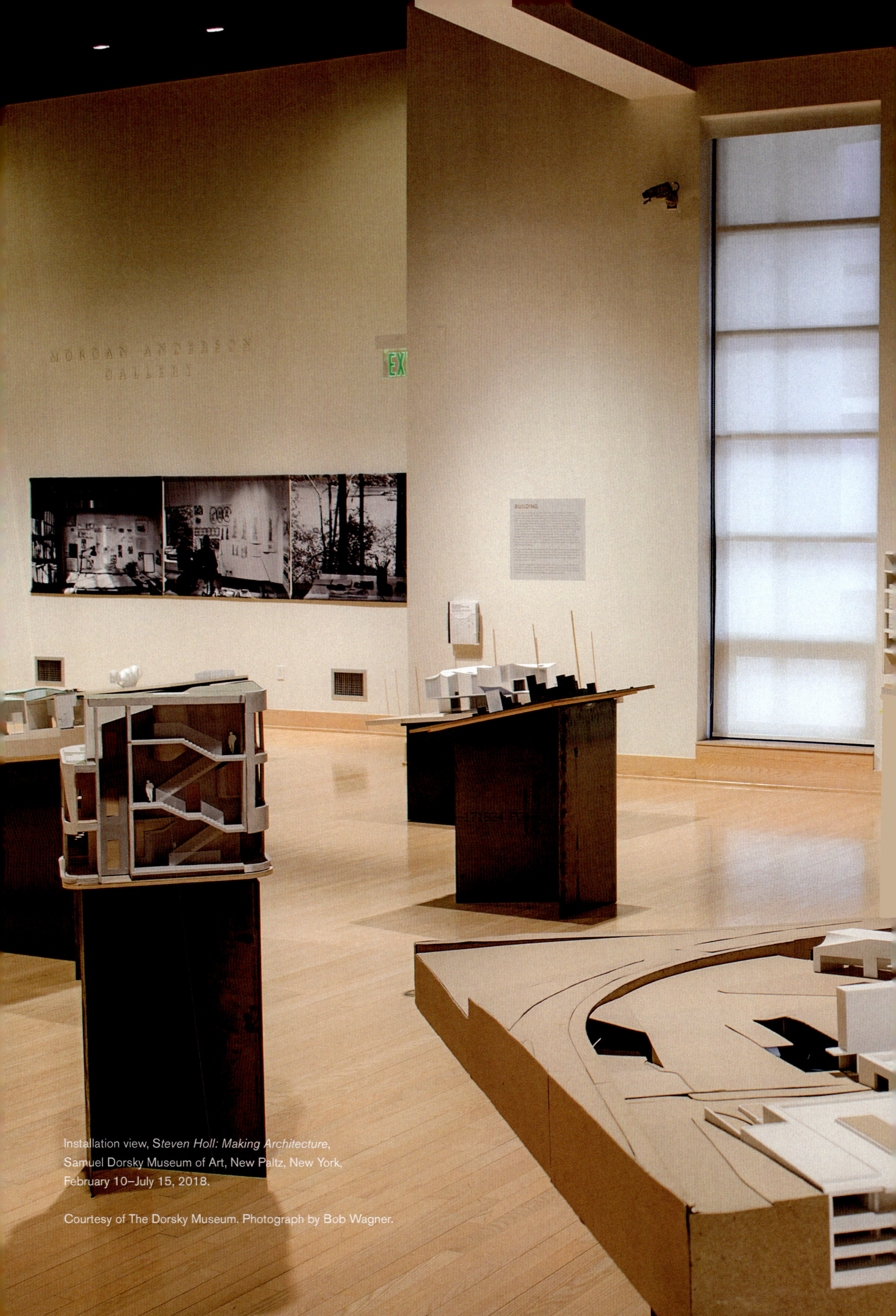

Installation view, *Steven Holl: Making Architecture*,
Samuel Dorsky Museum of Art, New Paltz, New York,
February 10–July 15, 2018.

Courtesy of The Dorsky Museum. Photograph by Bob Wagner.

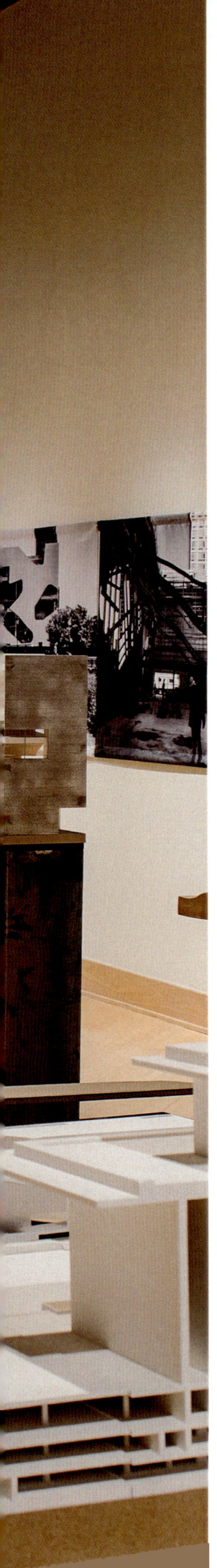

CURATOR'S ACKNOWLEDGMENTS

A considerable amount of time had passed since I had last seen Steven Holl when we met unexpectedly on the platform of the Rhinecliff train station, a special place on the bank of the Hudson River with views of the Catskill Mountains and the city of Kingston, early on a Monday morning in spring 2017. There I had the pleasure of meeting his wife, the architect Dimitra Tsachrelia, and their daughter, Io. Our initial discussion about an exhibition of Holl's work at the Dorsky Museum of Art happened on the Amtrak train we took together into New York City that morning. Subsequently I went to see Sara Pasti, Director of The Dorsky Museum, and from that moment, together with Steven and Dimitra, we began sharing ideas about the exhibition's curatorial focus.

This project has had a relatively short but deeply immersive gestation period leading up to the opening of the exhibition in February 2018 and the launch of this publication several months later. With a considerable body of work in his office nearing completion, we agreed to focus on how Holl makes architecture, giving particular credence to his remarkable drawings. It has been fascinating and illuminating for me to work in close collaboration with Steven and especially with Dimitra, who oversaw the exhibition on behalf of the Holl office, initially with Jacobo Mingorance Arranz and then with Raechel Root. The collaborative nature of this project has been especially rewarding, and has enhanced my thinking about curating architecture. The method of "Curating Holl" solidified when we finally moved away from a conventional organization by architectural project to a thematic structure that was guided by the network of thought that grounds Holl's architectural thinking. It was most rewarding to see how Dimitra brought the curatorial focus into the design of the exhibition. She also created the special display tables that enabled the juxtapositions of the unframed drawings. I am grateful to Raechel Root for the insight she brought to the collaboration, and for the myriad of ways she generously offered assistance. Early on, Julie Heffernan helped with the complicated

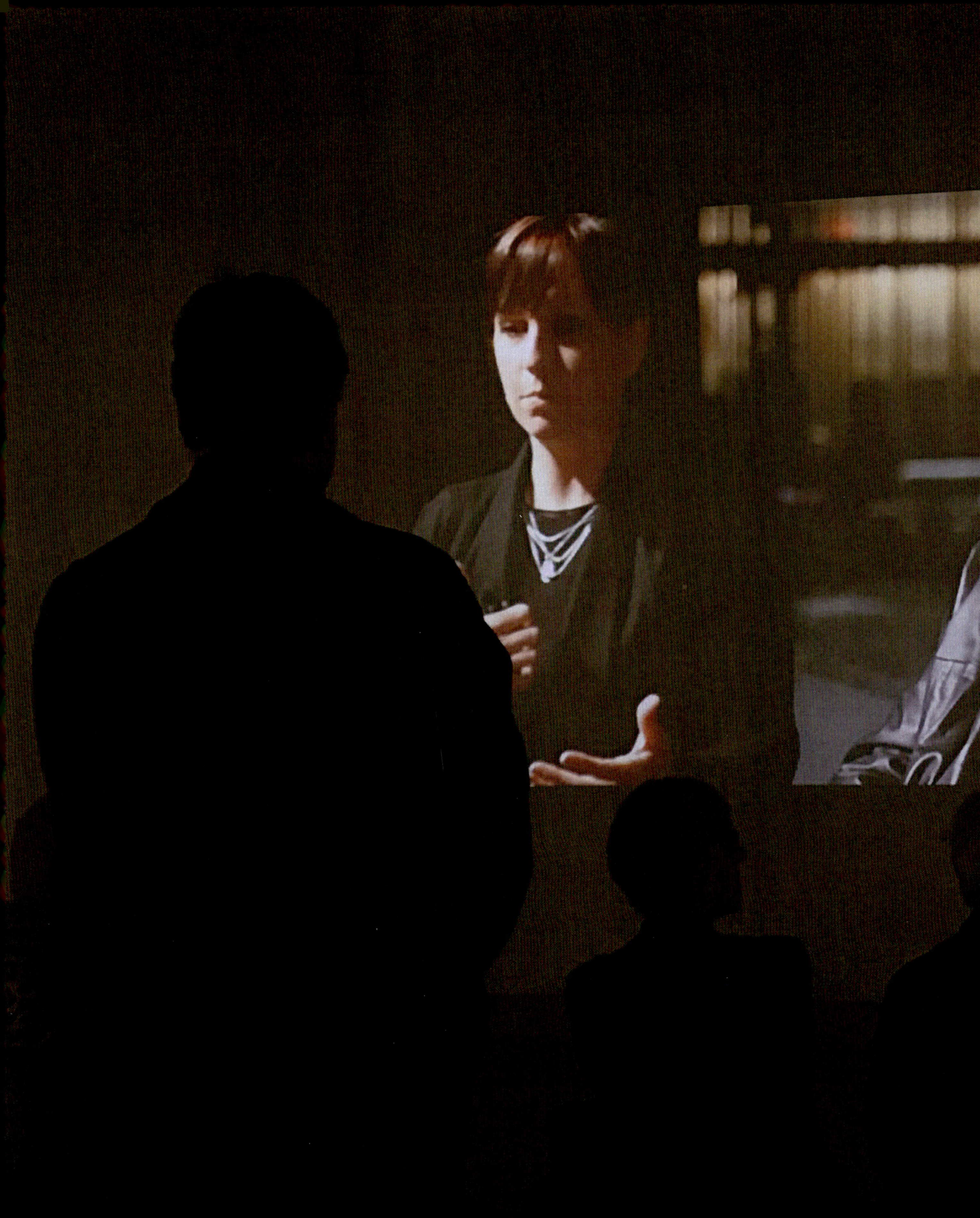

Installation view of *Dance with Architecture*, film,
Steven Holl: Making Architecture,
Samuel Dorsky Museum of Art, New Paltz, New York,
February 10–July 15, 2018.

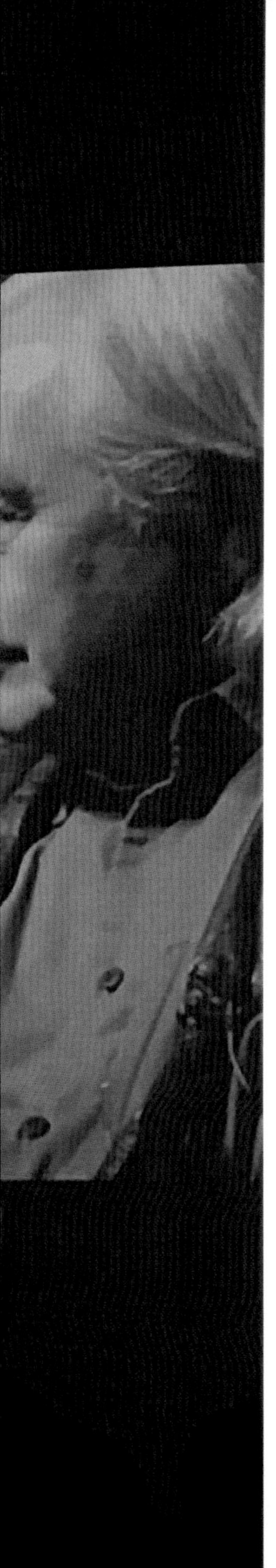

task of coordinating schedules. Suk Lee and Whitney Forward, architects in the Holl office, shared precious time with me looking at the Hunters Point Community Library and Lewis Center for the Arts.

I reiterate Sara Pasti's acknowledgments of State University of New York at New Paltz President Donald P. Christian and Provost and Vice President for Academic Affairs Lorin Basden Arnold for supporting this project. The Dorsky Museum of Art is a vibrant place that plays a major role in the cultural life of the Hudson Valley. Sara Pasti brings rigor, calm, and vision to the helm of the museum. Anastasia James joined the staff of the Dorsky as the exhibition was progressing. She was an enormous help with many details related to both the exhibition and this publication. A small staff comprised of creative and energetic people work behind the scenes at the Dorsky. I want to thank Wayne Lempka, Bob Wagner, and Janis Benincasa for the work they did on realizing the exhibition and related programs.

I also want to personally thank the contributors to this catalogue, Drs. Kerry Carso and Peter Olshavsky. Kristin Swan carefully and thoughtfully edited this volume. Jeff Lesperance conceived this beautifully designed book.

Finally I am grateful to Stuart Levine for his support and for our partnership, the ultimate collaboration in my life.

Nina Stritzler-Levine

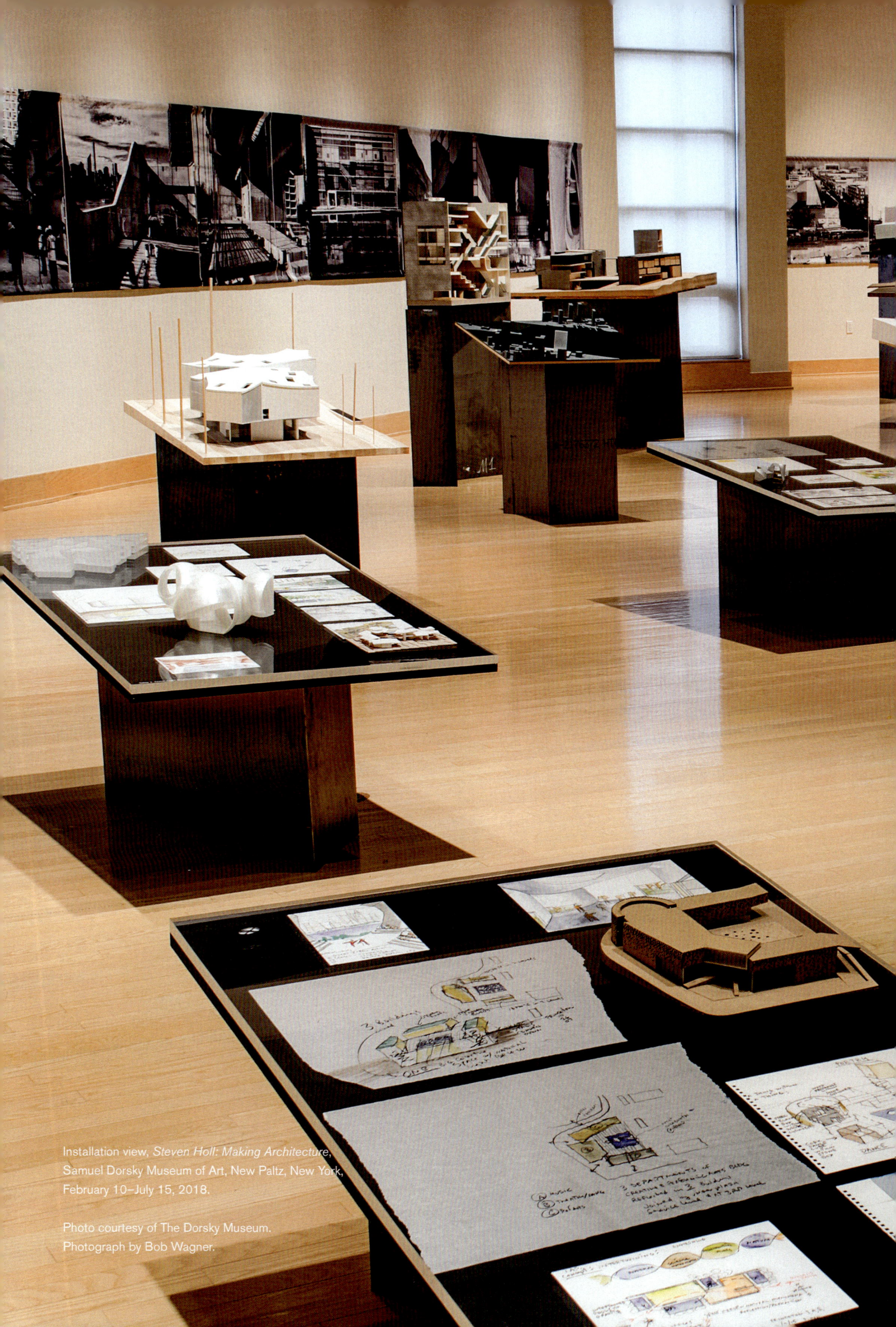

Installation view, *Steven Holl: Making Architecture*, Samuel Dorsky Museum of Art, New Paltz, New York, February 10–July 15, 2018.

Photo courtesy of The Dorsky Museum. Photograph by Bob Wagner.

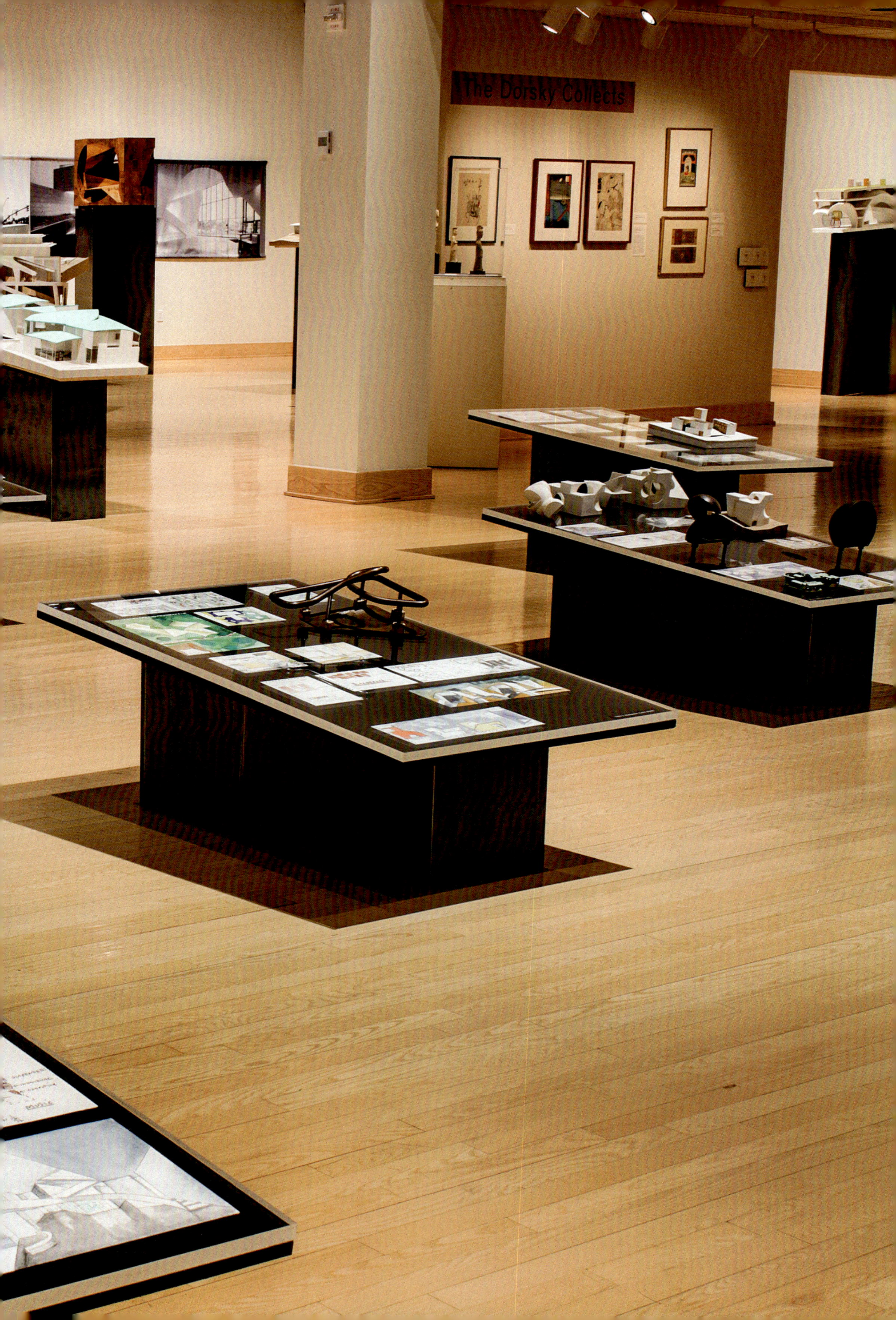
The Dorsky Collects

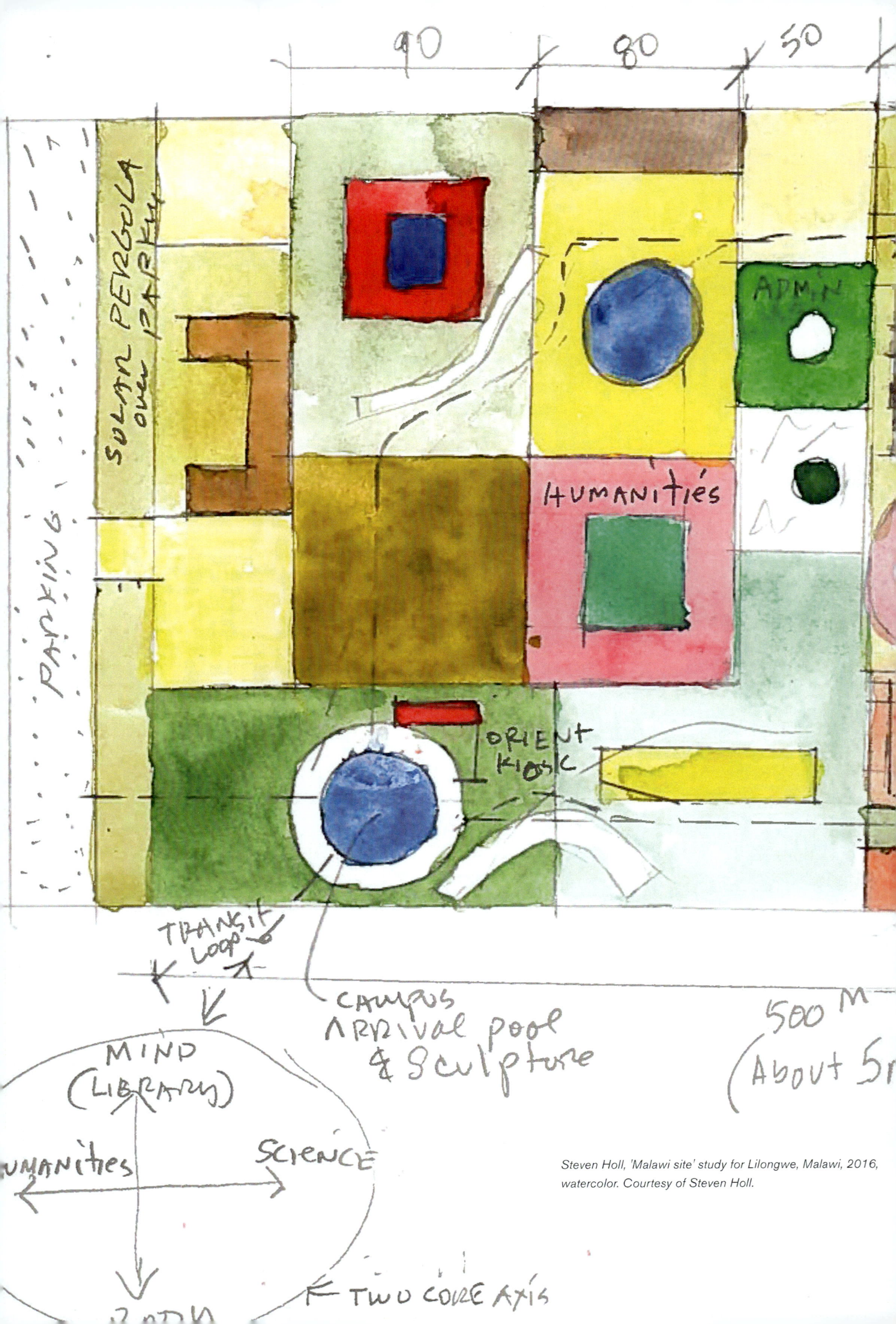

Steven Holl, 'Malawi site' study for Lilongwe, Malawi, 2016, watercolor. Courtesy of Steven Holl.

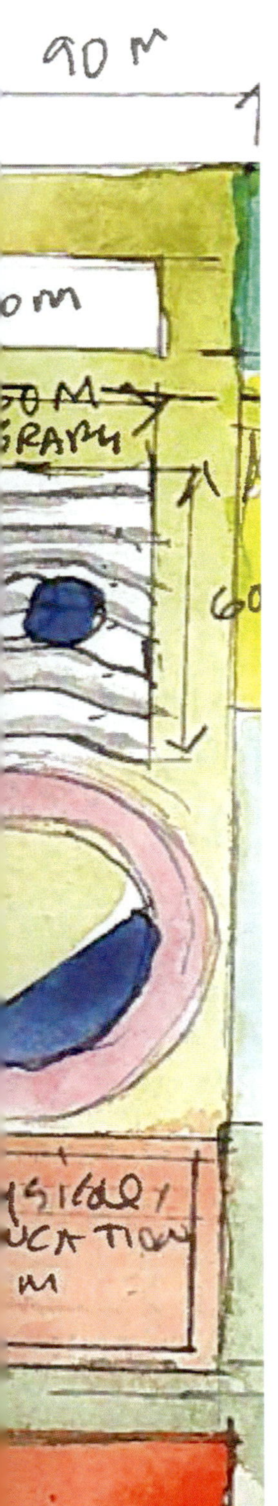

DRAWINGS AS THOUGHT

My 2-year-old daughter comes to me at dawn saying, "Drawing? Drawing?" She sees me making my morning watercolor and wants to get up on a chair with me and make drawings together. We draw sailboats, birds, airplanes—things she knows the words for. Her drawing of the moon, however, is not what we would recognize; rather, it is a long arabesque. She claims, "It's the moon; it's a moon-rabbit." The interaction of the hand and brain engages the human imagination in an immediate, neurologically connected way that cannot be replicated in a digital process.

I believe drawing, especially for architects, is a form of thought. Today, supercharged digital rendering techniques can depict a building in its proposed site in every detail—without an idea—without the thoughts of plans or sections.

The immediacy of a child's drawings brings us back to the beginning of thinking. The hand, the eye, the brain are all deeply connected when the child makes marks on paper, but the surprise—the imaginative creation of a "moon-rabbit"—that is the product of the mind. This deep, intuitive invention is the same for me as an old architect glancing back at 40 years of practice with 250 designs and 70 realized constructions. Each one of my architectural projects began as a drawing—usually a watercolor in a 5-by-7-inch watercolor tablet (more than 30,000 exist in my archive).

The drawings are thoughts in themselves, bringing together light, space, color, and a few words searching to define a concept. Many of these watercolors lead to dead ends, ideas that don't show promise—but I know this well and just keep drawing each day to search for the crucial idea that will drive a design.

In this exhibition, *Making Architecture*, organized by Nina Stritzler-Levine with exhibition design by Dimitra Tsachrelia, the drawings and models that are the primary tools for the beginning of architecture rise on steel "Z" bases through the galleries lined with a black-and-white photographic "frieze" showing stages of construction.

The flow of this sequence culminates in a room with short videos of the realized architectural works. This process is a joy, which I hope is embodied in the buildings for the enjoyment of future users.

Steven Holl

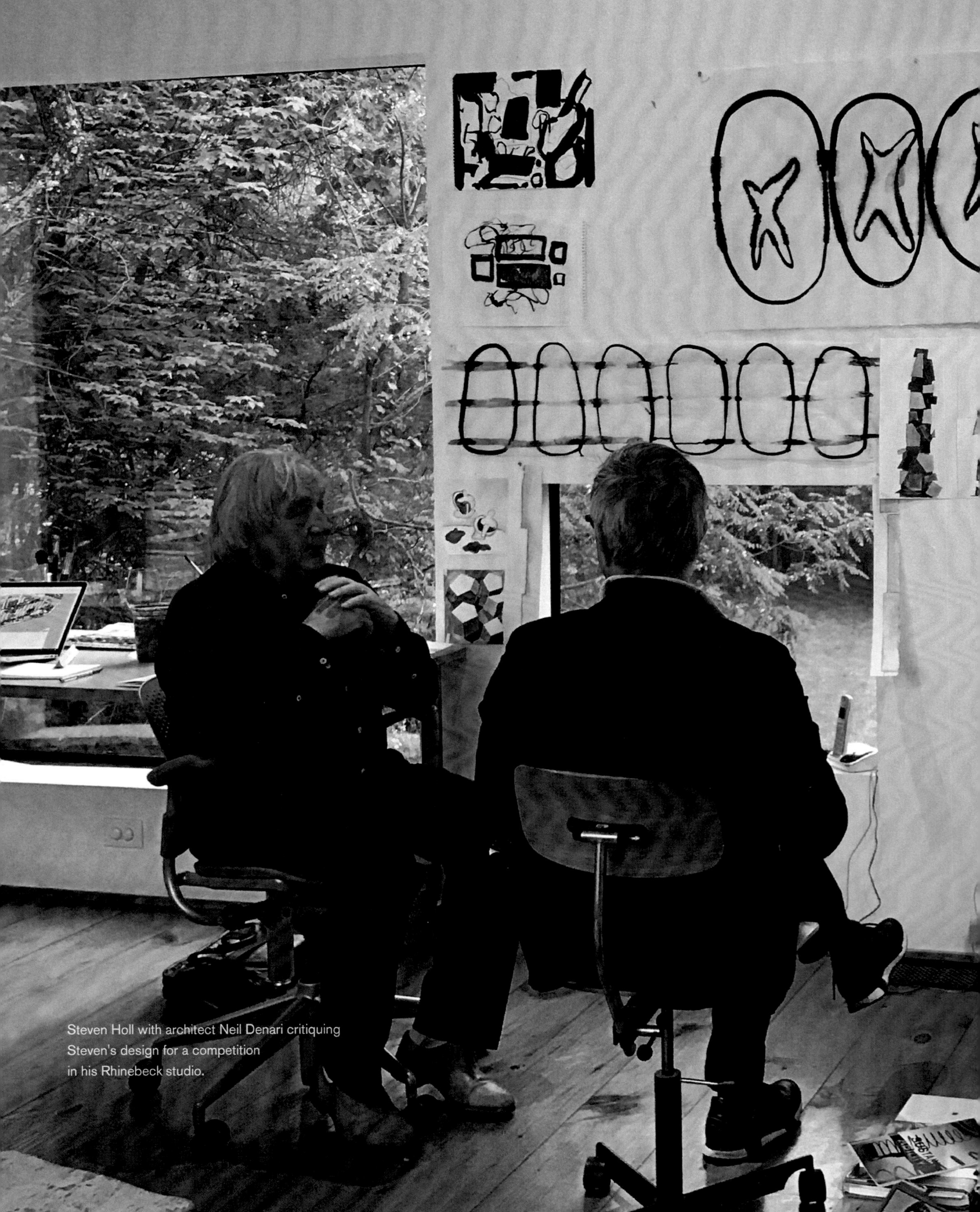

Steven Holl with architect Neil Denari critiquing Steven's design for a competition in his Rhinebeck studio.

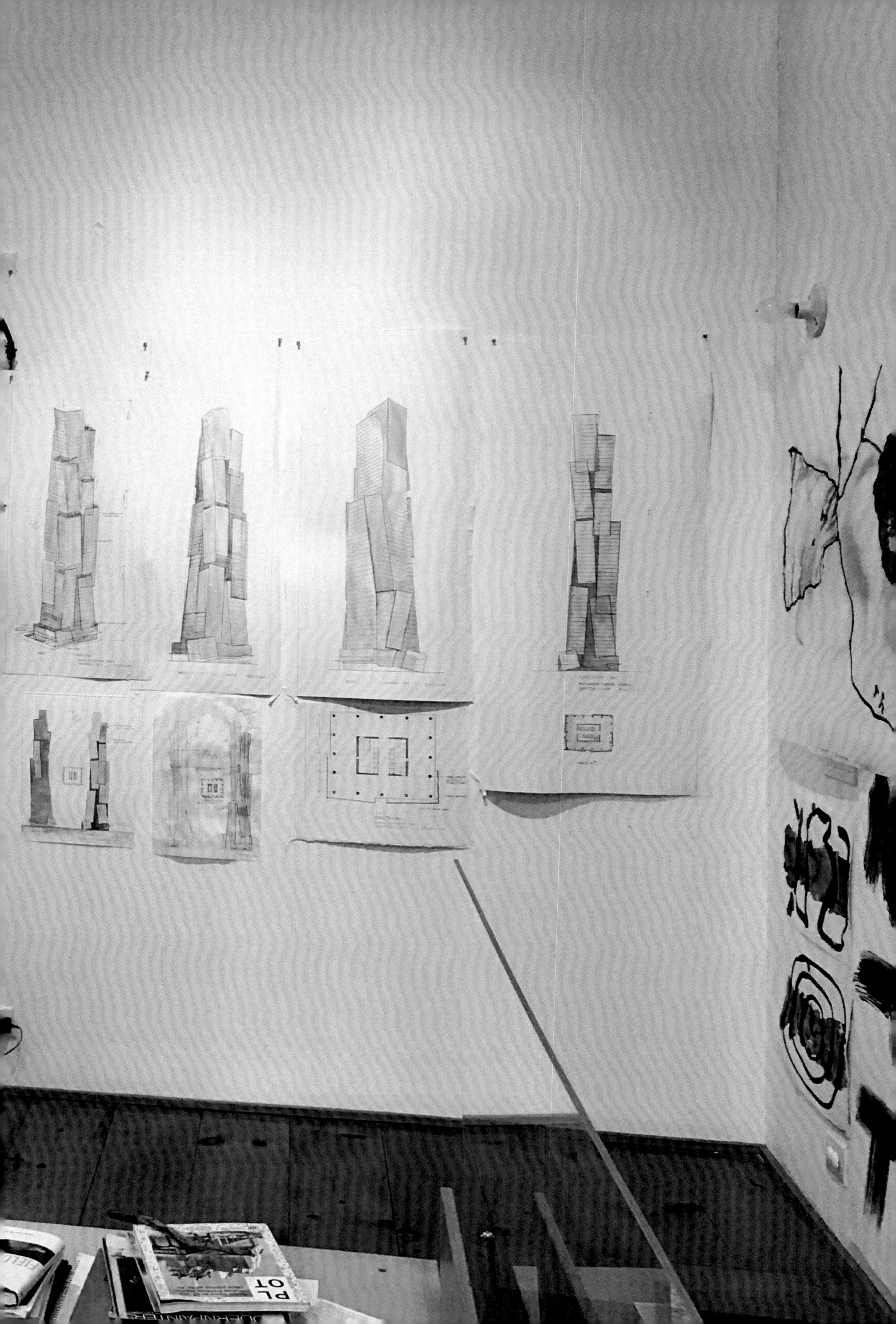

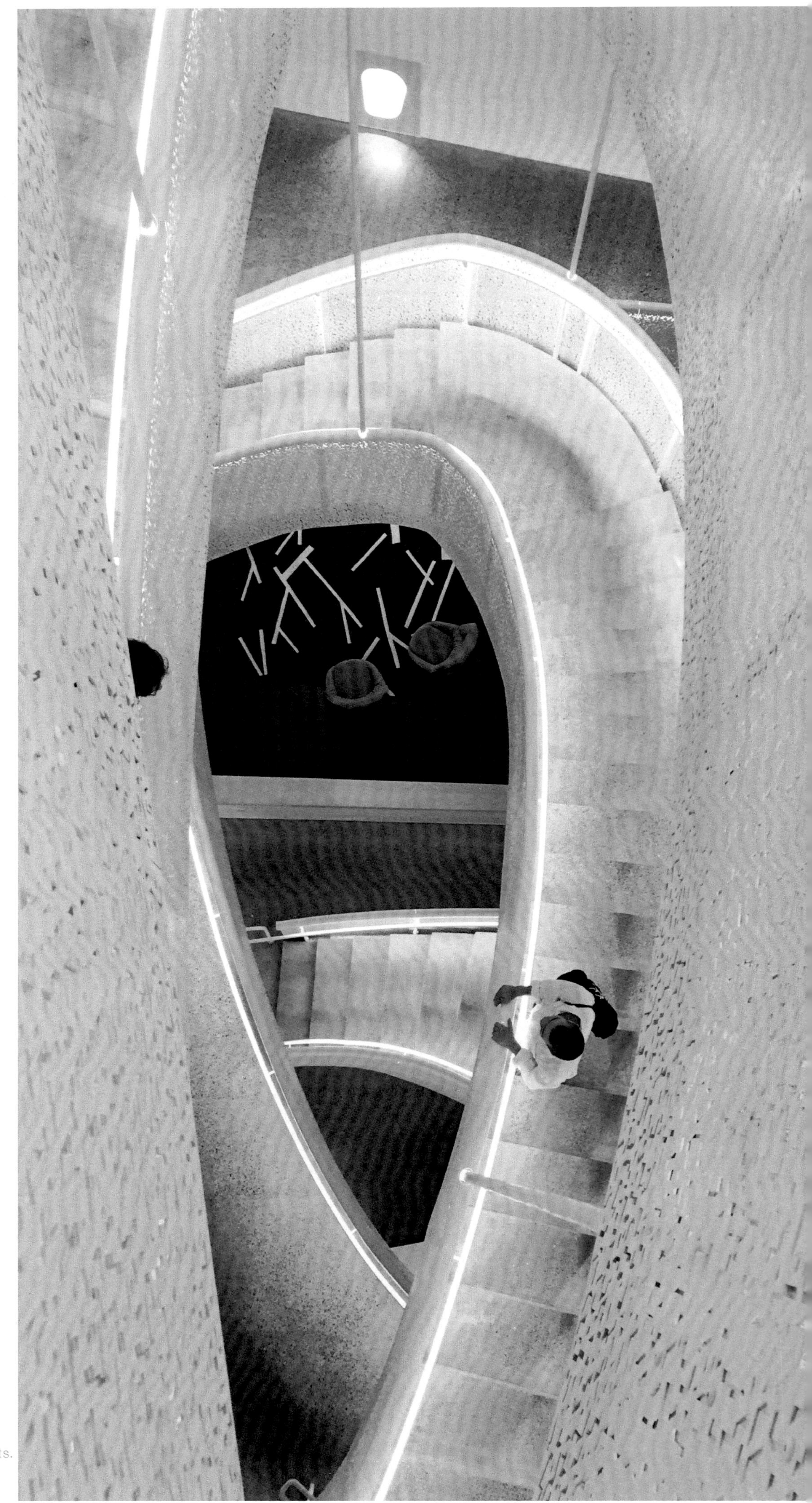

Steven Holl Architects,
"Dancing Stair," in the
Lewis Center for the Arts,
Princeton University,
Princeton, New Jersey, 2017.
Courtesy Steven Holl Architects.

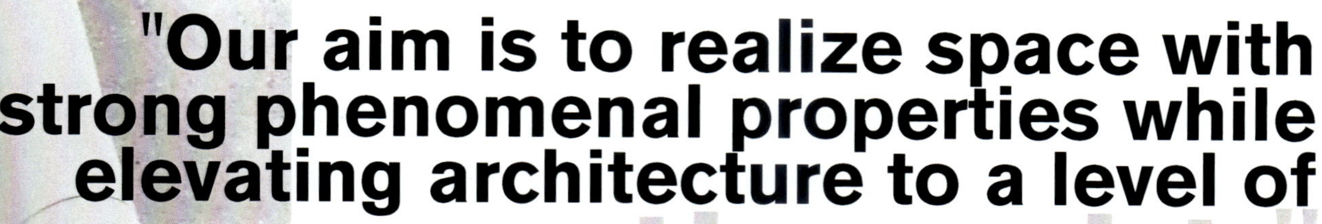

"Our aim is to realize space with strong phenomenal properties while elevating architecture to a level of thought."

MAKING ARCHITECTURE

Nina Stritzler-Levine

When Steven Holl wrote the statement above in 1996, he could not have imagined that such an aim, with its enduring debt to phenomenology, would prevail in what has become a global architecture practice. By phenomenal, the touchstone word in this statement, Holl meant that which is perceptible by all the senses. He seeks to enhance sensory experiences by shaping multiple architectural conditions: the positioning of a building in the landscape; the intertwining of physical space and natural light; the precise selection of seemingly ordinary design elements, such as stairs and ramps. Pursuant to the stated aim, he orchestrates the confluences of thought and phenomena, the mind and the senses.

As this catalogue and the exhibition at the Samuel Dorsky Museum of Art (fig. 1) that it accompanies seek to reveal, Holl's enduring aim is inextricably linked to his method of making architecture. The

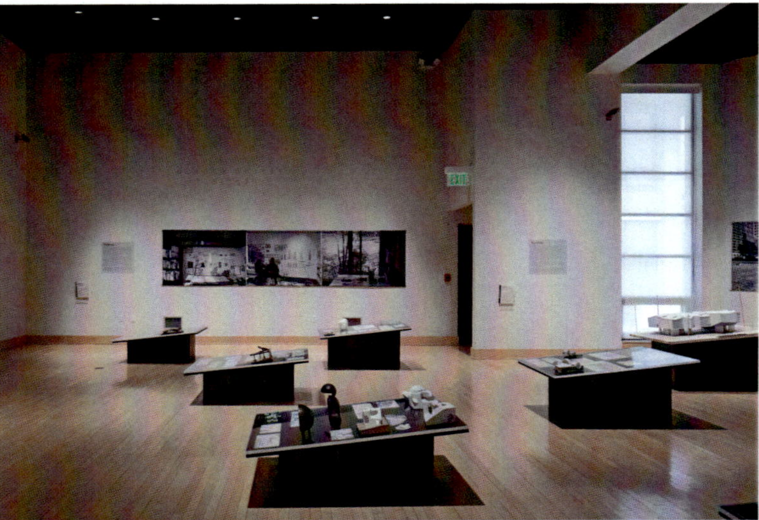

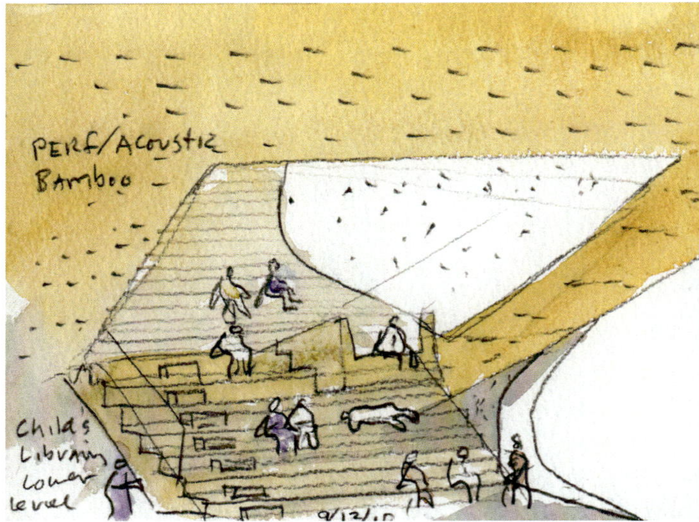

foundation of this method is drawing—almost always, drawing by hand. Alberto Pérez-Gómez has argued, "Value-laden tools of representation underlie the conception and realization of architecture."[1] That is certainly the case with Holl's choice of drawing by hand. Holl draws most often with watercolors in a standard 5 x 7 inch notebook. Reminiscent of the daily early morning painting and drawing routine followed by Le Corbusier, whose work he is known to greatly admire, Holl begins each day by drawing. With the stroke of a watercolor brush, a formative idea emerges on paper that anchors his architectural thinking. The washes of color and variations of transparency and opacity that can only be rendered with watercolors perhaps best express the sensory experience, the embodied spaces, Holl aims to realize.

The method of making architecture Holl follows has two interactive cycles.[2] The first—direct mind/hand/eye—connects formative ideas and the selection of architectural conditions and elements to the program. The second—work/drawing/word—privileges language, not only to communicate, but as an expression of thought. Most often and uncharacteristic of conventional architectural representations, Holl's drawings of interiors include an array of objects, even people (fig. 2). Others contain diagrams, a particular means of conveying architectural thinking. As Keith Albarn has explained:

> A diagram is the evidence of an idea being structured. It is not the idea itself but a model of it, intended to clarify characteristics or features of that idea. It is a form of communication, which

fig. 1

Installation view, *Steven Holl: Making Architecture*, Samuel Dorsky Museum of Art, New Paltz, New York, February 10–July 15, 2018.

fig. 2

Steven Holl, *Children's Library, Hunters Point Community Library*, Queens, New York, c. 2010, watercolor on paper. Courtesy of Steven Holl Architects.

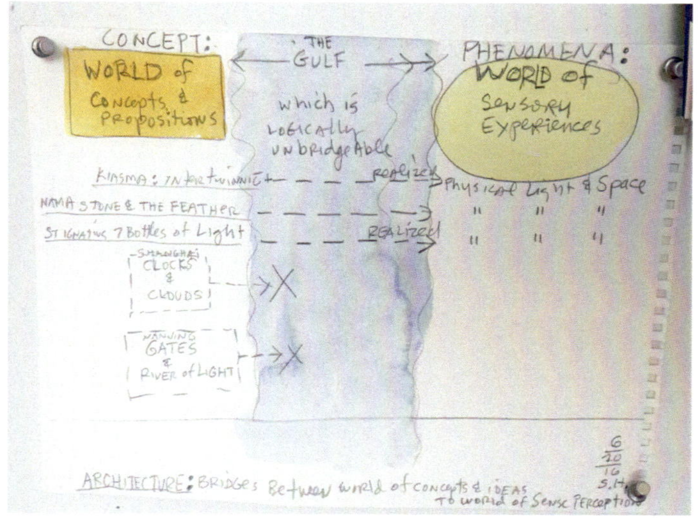

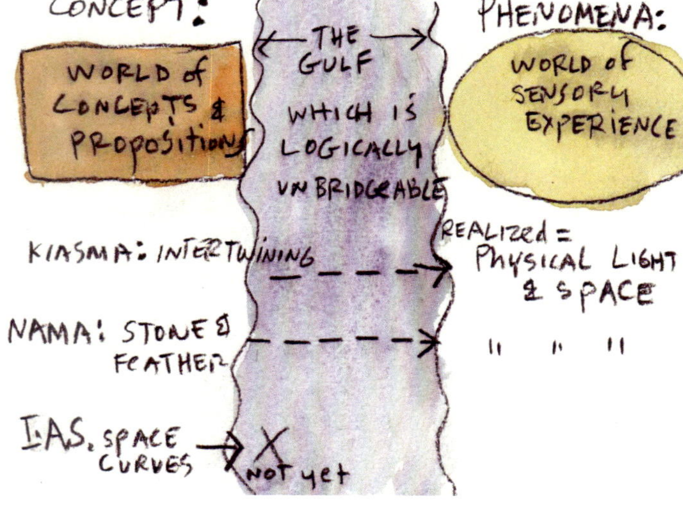

increases the pace of development, or allows an idea to function and develop for the thinker while offering the possibility of transferring it to others.[3]

In several of Holl's drawings, diagrams with words appear alone (fig. 3).[4] Ostensibly Holl makes these solely for his own use, rather than for a client or other architects on a project team. They engender a particular meaning to his overarching aim. This type of diagram identifies the guiding concept of a particular project, and most importantly, indicates whether the architectural conditions have achieved the phenomenological aim. For example, Holl annotated the column where the Institute for Advanced Studies (IAS), one of the current projects included in this catalogue, appears with the words "not yet" (fig. 4), because in its incomplete state he does not know if the space will actually have the phenomenal properties he seeks.

In the professional field of contemporary architecture in which Holl works, the potentialities of drawing have been fully exploited. However, today the computer is the primary tool used in this centuries-old practice. Daniel Libeskind was a pioneer in the conversion from drawing by hand to computer rendering. The late Zaha Hadid is perhaps the most well-known and gifted creator of such representations. Anthony Vidler has argued that the architects following this method of making architecture "shared an ironic sensibility that preferred the arbitrary rigor of an imposed and consciously subverted system to any emotive expressionism. Their drawings were cool and hard-line, black and white diagrams or functional forms."[5]

fig. 3

Steven Holl, *Concept and Phenomena I*, 2016, watercolor on paper. Photograph by Nina Stritzler-Levine.

fig. 4

Steven Holl, *Concept and Phenomena II*, n.d., watercolor on paper. Courtesy of Steven Holl Architects.

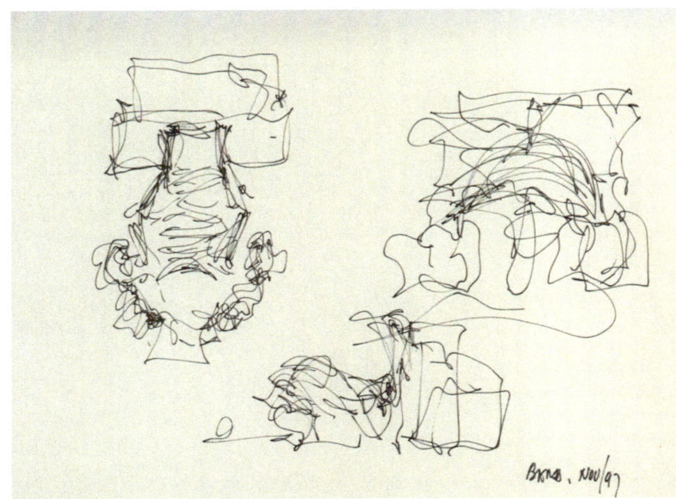

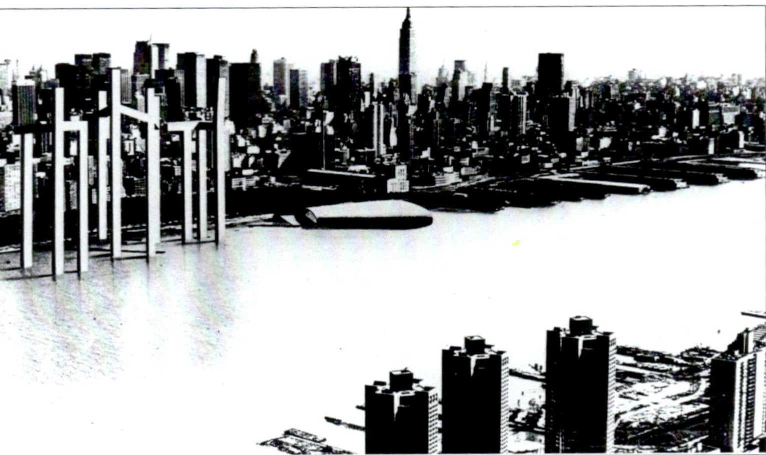

Such a description could not be more different from how or what Holl draws. He departs from the now essentially normative practice Vidler described by continuing to draw exclusively by hand. Holl is not alone in doing so. Frank Gehry, for example, has built his practice on this method (fig. 5).[6] Like Holl, he conceptualizes architecture while drawing by hand—but the similarities end there; the differences between Holl and Gehry are as deep as they are between Holl and architects who draw with computers. This line of demarcation is manifest in their contrasting aims. Gehry draws abstract configurations and densely contoured lines with ink on paper, which other architects in his office then extrapolate from to make computer renderings. The drawing is an initial gesture in the creation of architectural form. For Holl, in contrast, drawing is how he depicts the emotive expressionism of physical space that Vidler argued was precisely what architects using computers invariably work against. Holl draws to create and then expand upon a particular system of thought that guides his projects through each phase of the complex process of making architecture. Holl, in fact, considers the computer to be a deterrent to architectural thinking, especially during the formative conceptual stage of a project. But this does not mean he is adverse to technology. On the contrary, Holl exploits the full potential of technology in many of his projects. His concerns are with the cognitive

fig. 5

Frank Gehry, Fisher Center for the Performing Arts, Bard College, Annandale-on-Hudson, New York, November, 1977, ink on paper. Gehry Partners.

fig. 6

Steven Holl with Peter Lynch, Romain Ruther, and Stephen Cassell, *Edge of a City, Parallax Towers Project*, New York, New York, 1990, wood and paper.

disconnection that he believes results when a computer instead of the hand is used to draw. He draws by hand foremost to "activate the brain"—to stimulate the synaptic connections that enhance creativity.[7]

Holl arrived in New York City from his native Washington State in 1976, and opened his practice the following year. The story of his determination to establish and sustain an idea-driven architectural practice while New York City was in a deep economic downturn is well known.[8] During the protracted period of expectancy to design his first major public building, which finally came in 1993 when he won the competition for the Museum of Contemporary Art (called Kiasma) in Helsinki,[9] Holl had enough work to keep his small office going. The late Lebbeus Woods, who was one of Holl's oldest friends and conversationalists on architecture, summed it up best when he explained: "Being demanding and uncompromising with his clients in pursuit of the realization of his concepts made it close to impossible for him to build much during the first twenty-five years of his practice."[10]

Holl made professional advances in parallel practices as well. In the early years he created visionary projects, of which the Bronx Gymnasium Bridge (1977) and Edge of a City projects (1989–90) are the most celebrated (fig. 6). Lacking a proper vehicle for disseminating his architectural ideas, in 1978 he founded and published the journal *Pamphlet Architecture* with the San Francisco-based bookseller William Stout. It became an outlet for Holl's prolific writing on architecture, as well as for other architects of his generation.[11] As an emerging architect, Holl also began teaching studio classes—eventually becoming a tenured member of the Columbia School of Architecture faculty—thanks to James Polshek, then dean of the school. Recently Holl demonstrated his ongoing commitment to architectural pedagogy as an investigatory practice by teaching his first architecture history and theory seminar, where he encouraged his students to draw by hand and to think of themselves as architect-artists in the tradition of Frank Lloyd Wright and Le Corbusier.[12]

When the Museum of Modern Art in New York City organized the exhibition *Emilio Ambasz / Steven Holl: Architecture* in 1989, it was clear Holl was gaining recognition and stature.[13] Today it is relatively common for art museums to mount exhibitions on emerging architects, but receiving this opportunity at that time was unusual. The exhibition focused on Holl's residential commissions and a few competition projects, like Amerika-Gedenkbibliothek in Berlin. A review by Paul Goldberger, then architecture critic for the *New York Times*, insisted Holl's work "tapped into our deepest moods and feelings." Holl was not just a gifted designer, he was "an architect deeply concerned with finding a point at which the deepest and most powerful currents of architectural experience can be put to the service of social and urbanistic needs."[14]

The Dorsky Museum's *Steven Holl: Making Architecture* considers eleven projects, most of which will not be completed until 2019. This body of mature work evokes the concerns and larger purpose Goldberger thought to be evident already in the architect's work three decades ago. However, now the geographic and programmatic diversity is far greater.[15] Today professional challenges continue as one would think they would for an architect still unwilling to accept work that would

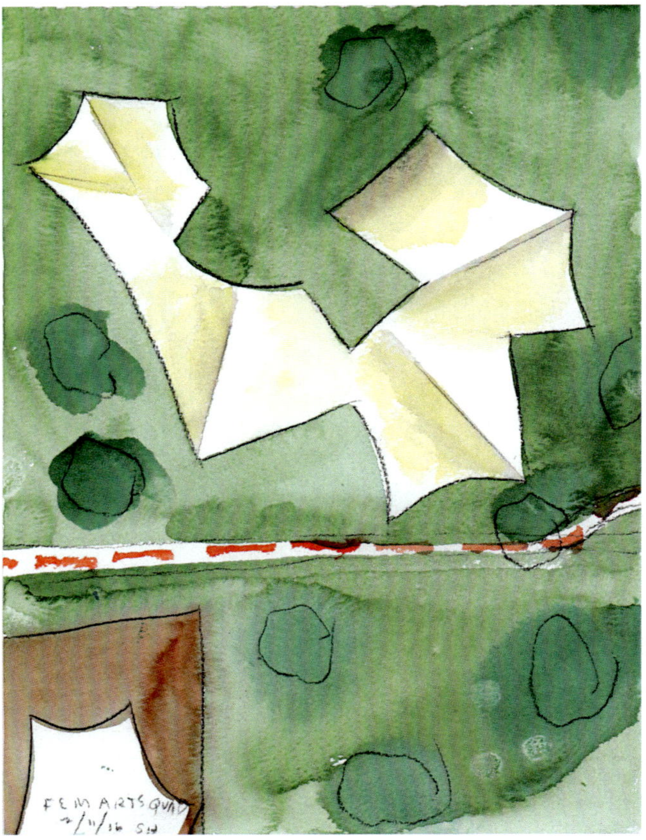

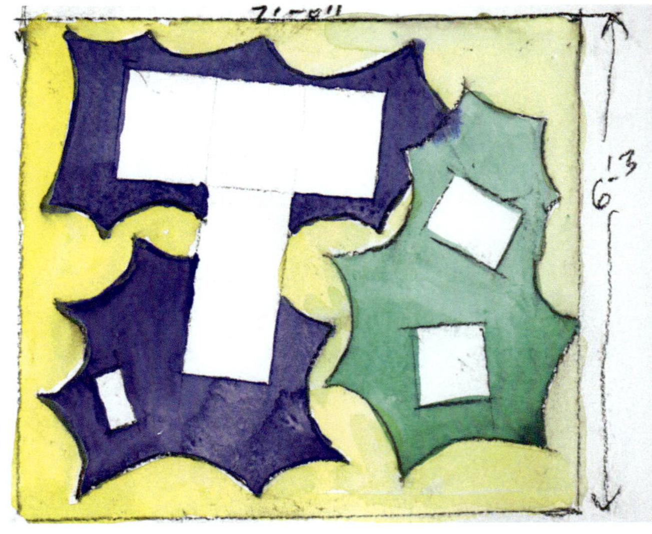

compromise his aim and acute sensibilities. The primary struggle for Holl is to be true to his convictions in the face of success. Clients from different sectors worldwide seek him out, desiring the conceptual depth in architecture that had been a hindrance to Holl receiving public commissions in the early days of his career.

Indicative of the particular client-architect relationships Holl is nurturing are comments made in a recent interview by Robyn Piggott, who is leading the team working with Holl on the Arts Building at Franklin & Marshall College in Lancaster, Pennsylvania. Piggott described the advantages of working with an architect who "got the visual arts," who pushed the administrators and faculty to create architecture or a building that was more than a better facility. Holl proposed the building team at Franklin & Marshall "recombine disciplines and create a visual arts center that encourages engagement among the students and faculty working in different disciplines rather than just a Fine Arts building." Most importantly, Piggott admired the research and careful study Holl made of the campus and the site, especially the distinctive trees and landscape. The early drawings show how he changed the orientation of the geometry to accentuate the trees and to capture the light (figs. 7 and 8).[16] This telling narrative about

fig. 7

Steven Holl, *F&M Arts Quad*, Arts Building, Franklin & Marshall College, Lancaster, Pennsylvania, 2016, watercolor on paper. Courtesy of Steven Holl Architects.

fig. 8

Steven Holl, *Study*, Arts Building, Franklin & Marshall College, Lancaster, Pennsylvania, 2016, watercolor on paper. Courtesy of Steven Holl Architects.

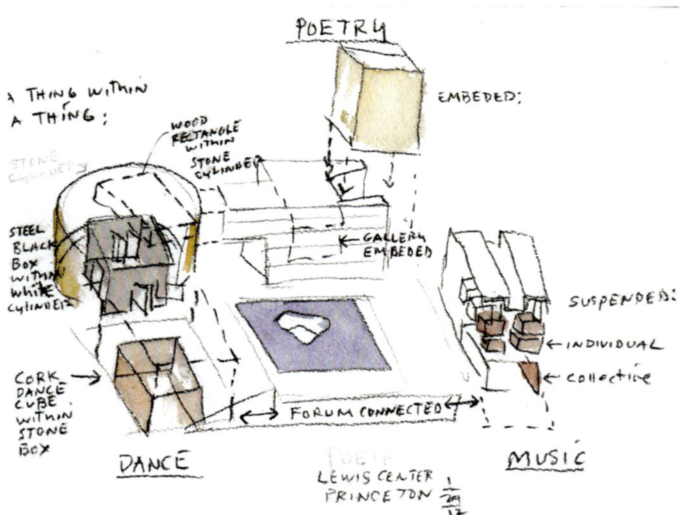

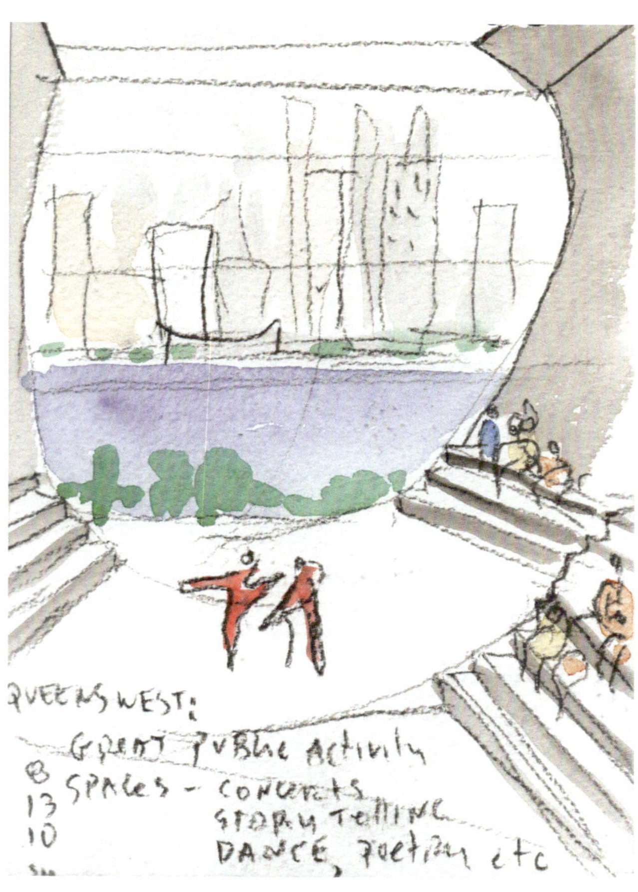

Holl urging the client to think beyond the prescribed program exemplifies what I call Holl's macro-aims. In this case it was creating space he describes as a "social condenser," a term adopted from Russian Constructivist discourse. In the Franklin & Marshall project he created community spaces where students and faculty working within different disciplines can interact, and where the physical spaces encourage interdisciplinary activities. The Lewis Center for the Arts and the Hunters Point Community Library included in this catalogue have spaces conceived with a similar spatial/social idea that Holl brought to the client (figs. 9 and 10).[17]

It is well known that drawing by hand with watercolors is the basis of how Holl makes architecture. Below I elaborate on the specific places where he draws, and on the method of making architecture Holl describes as an "abstract journey," where the cycles of making architecture described earlier happen. Holl's particular workplaces are the loci of his "value-laden" architectural thinking. The principal spaces, one in midtown Manhattan and the other in Rhinebeck, two hours north of New York City in the Hudson Valley, are ateliers, or artist studios. The places are signifiers of the architect-artist.[18]

fig. 9

Steven Holl, *Dance, Poetry and Music*, Lewis Center for the Arts, Princeton University, Princeton, New Jersey, 2012, watercolor on paper. Courtesy of Steven Holl Architects.

fig. 10

Steven Holl, *Social Condenser*, Hunters Point Community Library, Queens, New York, 2010, watercolor on paper. Courtesy of Steven Holl Architects.

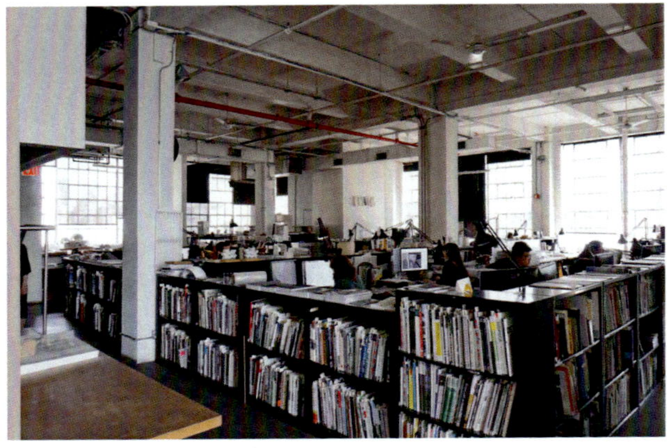

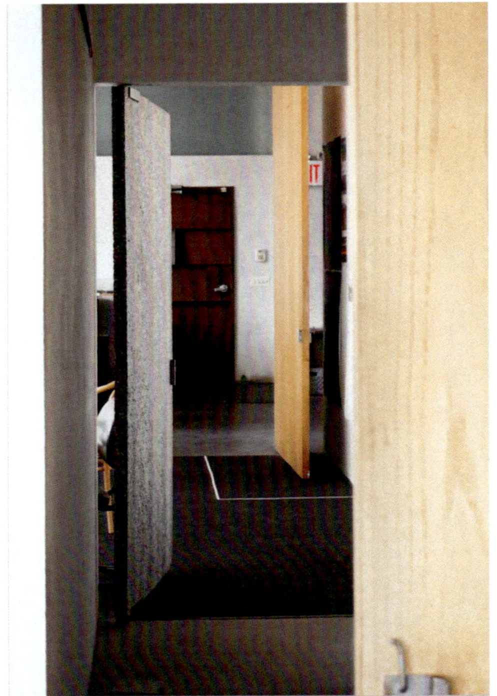

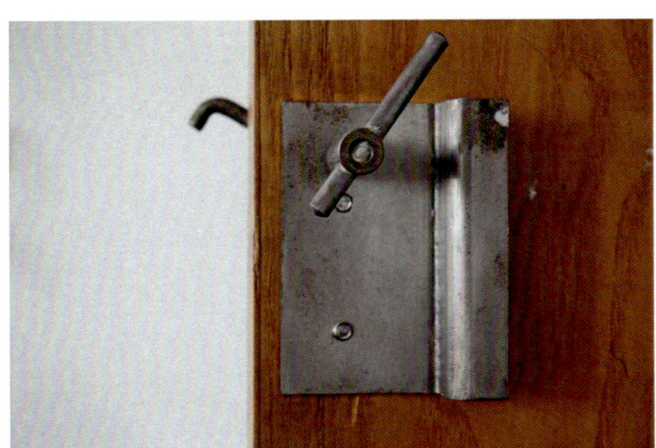

Kerry Dean Carso's "In Union with the Land: Hudson Valley Traditions and Steven Holl's Architecture" provides unprecedented thoughts on the connections in Holl's architecture to the acclaimed artists of the Hudson River School. Carso positions Holl within a tradition of artists with deep connections to the awe-inspiring natural landscape of the Hudson Valley, where he has resided for more than twenty years.

To further elucidate the lines of connectivity in Holl's work between architecture and philosophy, Peter Olshavsky's essay in this volume, "Reconfiguring Architectural Agency," considers how philosophy—particularly phenomenology—informs Holl's architectural thinking. Olshavsky argues that this connection is a form of agency for enhancing everyday life.

The Projects section that follows these chapters connects this catalogue with the curatorial thinking behind the exhibition at The Dorsky Museum. It includes descriptions of the eleven projects that are the focus of the exhibition; the exhibition checklist, which corresponds with the organization of the installation; and photographs of the installation. Designed by Dimitra Tsachrelia in collaboration with the Steven Myron Holl Foundation, the installation derived from our investigation of ways to exhibit the systems of thought depicted in Holl's drawings across the different projects. Most importantly, instead of hanging the drawings on the wall in frames as they are seen in most exhibitions, we moved them

fig. 11

Interior view of Steven Holl Architects, New York, New York, 2017. Courtesy of Steven Holl Architects.

fig. 12

Interior view of Steven Holl Architects, New York, New York, 2017. Courtesy of Steven Holl Architects.

fig. 13

Steven Holl, *Conference Room Door*, prototype, door handle, May 2018. Photograph by Jacobo Mingorance, courtesy of Steven Holl Architects.

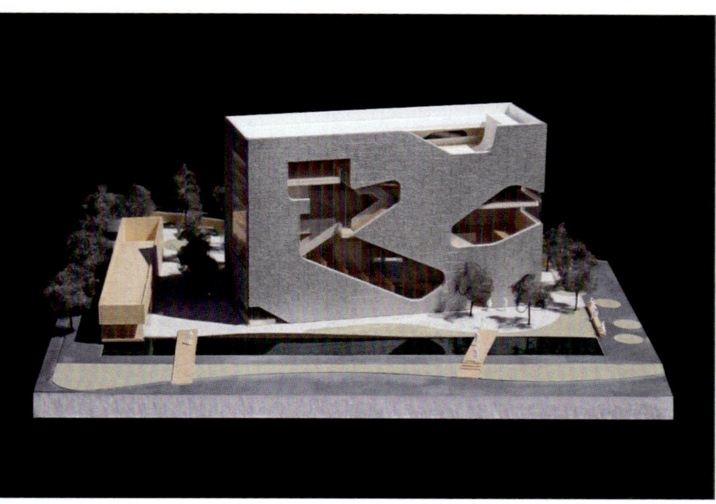

to the center of the gallery on display tables Tsachrelia designed.

TWO ATELIERS

The New York City office of Steven Holl architects is located in a building on West 31st Street, midway between the multiple exit and entrance lanes of the Lincoln Tunnel and Tenth Avenue in Manhattan. Twenty years ago, when Holl moved there from downtown Hudson Street, most of the surrounding buildings that had once been factories were derelict, and the kind of urban disenfranchisement that tends to develop around major transit hubs pervaded the area. Today, on what was a rare parcel of open land adjacent to Holl's office on Tenth Avenue, known as the Hudson Rail Yards, the most ambitious urban development project in the history of New York City is underway.[19] Now large numbers of pedestrians scurry along Tenth Avenue, seemingly dwarfed by the emerging monumental luxury skyscrapers, dodging the inescapable traffic entering and exiting the tunnel.[20] As a visitor to Steven Holl Architects, what is most striking about this rapidly changing urban landscape is the contrast between the cacophony outside and the silent yet visibly active office inside. One experiences a welcome sense of relief upon entering a place where the palpable silence contrasts with the frenetic street below.

At the southwest corner of the office, well hidden from the entrance, and strategically separated from the fifty or so architects who occupy workstations in the main open-plan space (fig. 11), is Holl's private workspace. This and the adjacent conference room are the only places in the office with doors (fig. 12). Holl designed the doors as prototypes that reveal the materiality of his practice and the ingenious hanging mechanisms and hardware (fig. 13) he makes in the tradition of other architects he admires, particularly Alvar Aalto. These architectural details and the models that are prominently displayed there evoke the laboratory spirit of the office. Holl uses models to generate ideas (fig. 14). They are how he experiments with materials, and methods of construction. The hand-technology dichotomy that is very much a part of Holl's architectural thinking is evident in the model-making area located across the open-plan space from where Holl works. Most of the models made there are constructed and reworked many times by hand until the right

fig. 14

Steven Holl Architects, *Model*, Hunters Point Community Library, Queens, New York, 2010, wood, cork, acrylic, and steel wool. Courtesy of Steven Holl Architects.

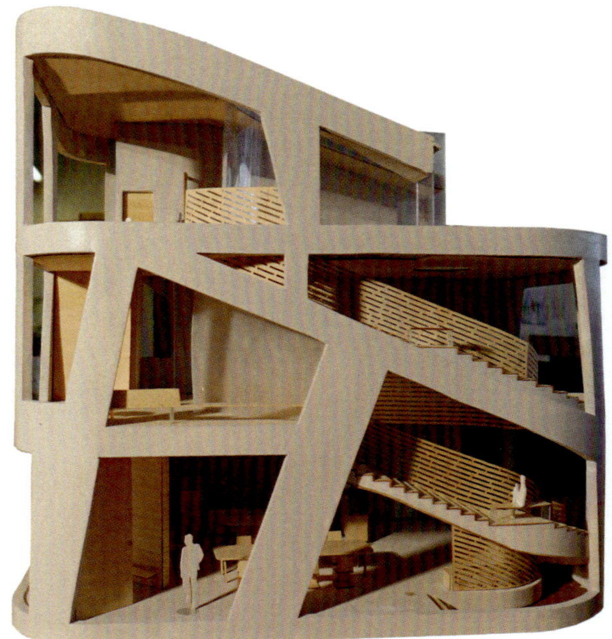

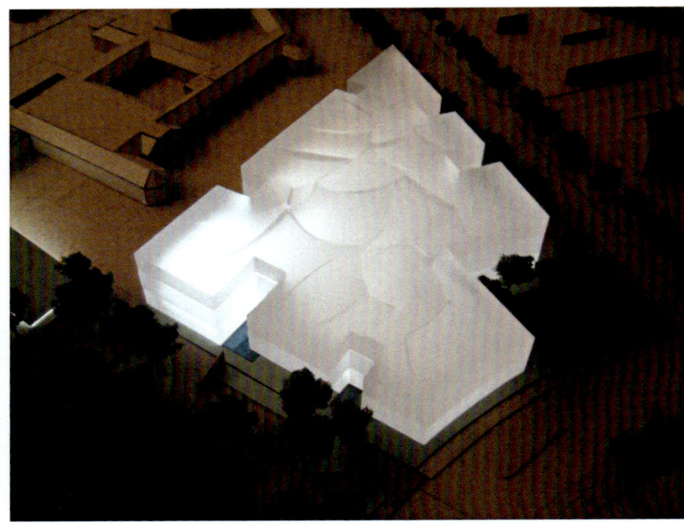

solution to a design problem is found (fig. 15). Others appear fully formed from digital printing machines and (fig.16).

Returning to Holl's secluded workspace, this is where the hand/technology dichotomy that eventually synthesizes in the design phase of a project is most vividly apparent. *Atelier*, the French word for an artist's studio, best describes this space. That is the word Le Corbusier, the most prominent architect-artist used for his office.[21] Holl's atelier is where formative ideas emerge, where the idea shapes and is shaped by the program. Upon entering the atelier, one encounters an expansive and rather curious view of downtown Manhattan from the large window wall (fig. 17). Except for the single tower of the new World Trade Center faintly seen in the far distance, the characteristic skyscrapers that form the recognizable skyline of Manhattan are mostly absent. The buildings seen from these windows are quite low, much lower than the massive skyscrapers emerging nearby on Tenth Avenue. The drenching sunlight that floods the space illuminates the assortment of objects, mostly models, on the shelf in front of the window. The transparent surfaces of the digitally printed models stand out against the skyline. A globe perches there as well, perhaps to show exactly where Holl is building on four continents. Books on architecture line the shelves on the walls next to and beneath the windows. This is one of several places in the office where Holl keeps his extensive library, which he uses in his research. Holl uses art and architectural history to develop new ideas.

fig. 15

Steven Holl, *Study Model*, Maggie's Cancer Care Centre, London, England, 2011, resin-impregnated plaster 3D print, plywood, and acrylic. Courtesy of Steven Holl Architects.

fig. 16

Steven Holl Architects, *Model, Canopy of Light*, Museum of Fine Arts, Houston, 2011, CNC milled acrylic, sanded. Courtesy of Steven Holl Architects.

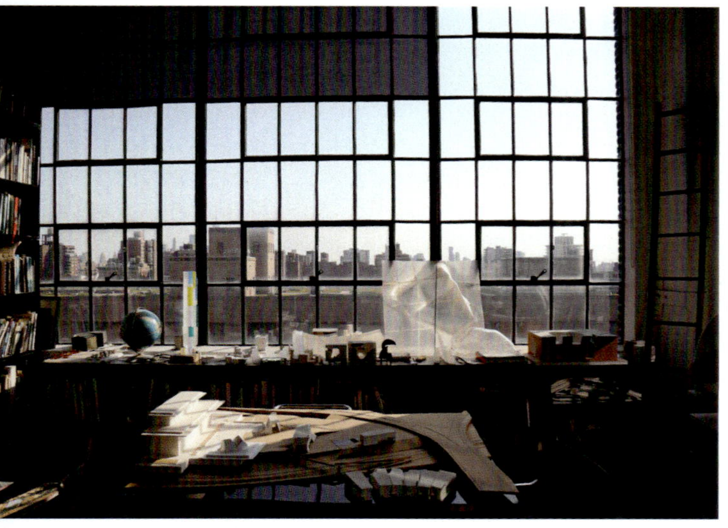

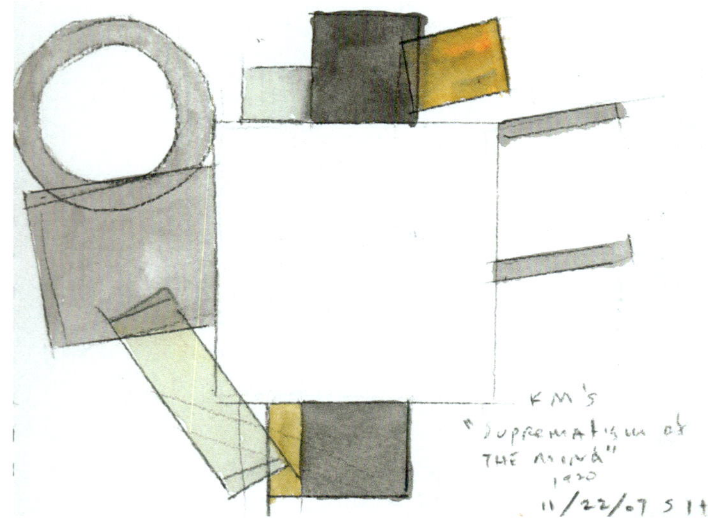

The current body of work references many precursors to his thinking, from Michelangelo to Malevich (fig. 18).

The meaning and defining of this space as an atelier is best understood from the other side of the room, where Holl works at a table designed, in all of its simplicity, especially for drawing by hand (fig. 19). The computer, the omnipresent tool of an architect today—including at the desks of the other architects in Holl's office—is out of sight. Parallel bar and canisters of pencils and other traditional hand tools are carefully arranged and waiting to be used, as is the open and well-worn box of watercolors, the essential tool of this architect-artist. On the north wall above the table are two shelves lined with sketchbooks, some in archival boxes. While drawing new concepts

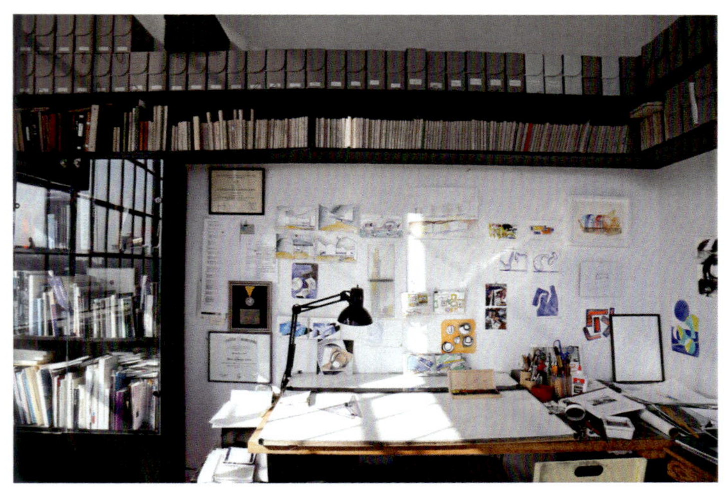

fig. 17

Interior view, Steven Holl's atelier, facing south, Steven Holl Architects, New York, New York, 2017. Courtesy of Steven Holl Architects.

fig. 18

Steven Holl, *Suprematism of the Mind*, Lewis Center for the Arts, Princeton University, Princeton, New Jersey, 2007, watercolor on paper. Courtesy of Steven Holl Architects.

fig. 19

Interior view, Steven Holl's atelier, facing north, Steven Holl Architects, New York, New York, 2017. Courtesy of Steven Holl Architects.

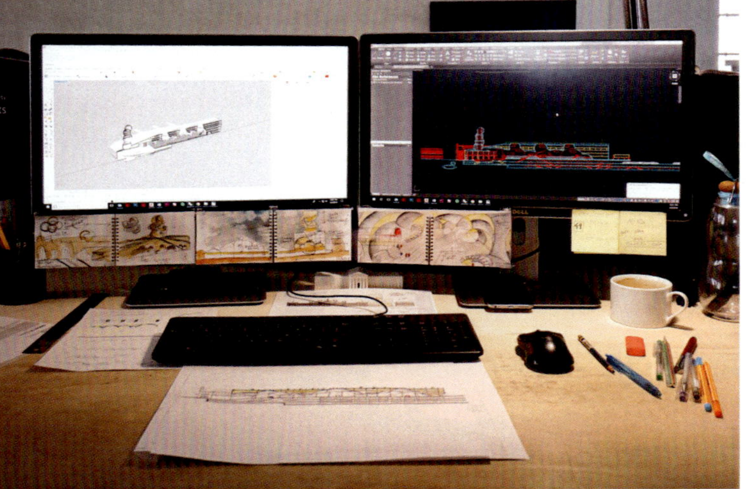

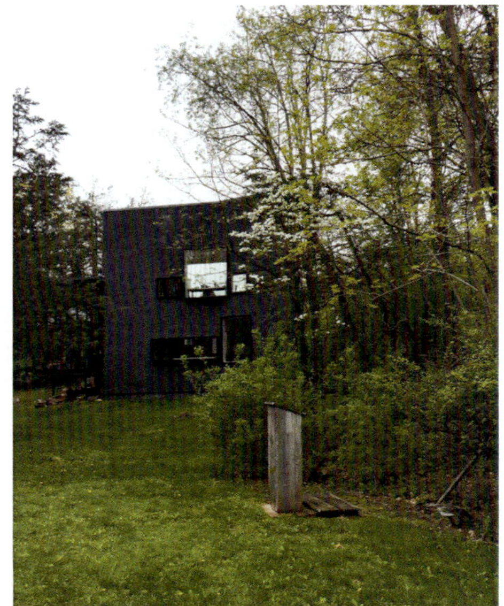

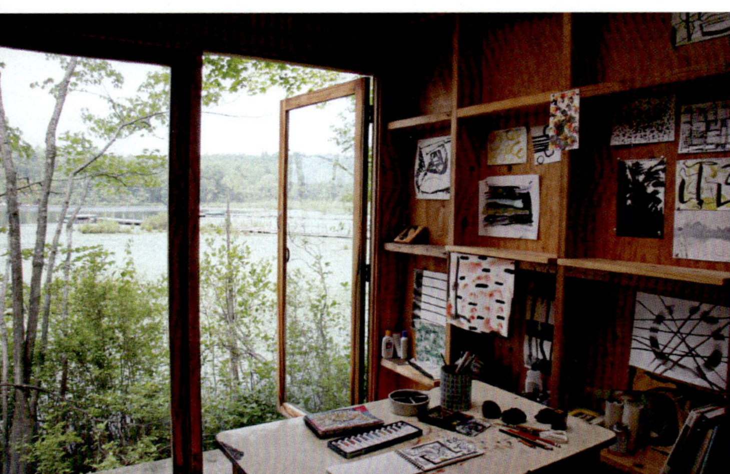

for current projects, Holl refers to these earlier drawings; they are kept nearby to be used as conceptual points of reference from the past, like the books in his library. These are moments in his own architectural history that inform his current work. Photographs, diplomas, and drawings for new and yet-to-be-completed projects are tacked up on the board above the table in a carefully arranged collage of images.

As I wandered around the main open-plan space outside Holl's office, where architects at computer stations were working on a myriad of projects, I realized just how critical Holl's drawings are to making architecture. At the workstation of an architect creating axonometric drawings for the Oceanic Pavilion, CinPaoSan Necropolis in Taiwan there were six watercolors taped to the bottom of two computer screens (fig. 20). This act of transference from Holl's watercolors to the computer rendering is what separates making architecture in Holl's office from the normative and arguably rote practice of working directly on computers that happens in architects' offices across New York City, and around the world. I immediately understood this transference was more than an extrapolation of the representation. The transference of an idea Holl develops during the critical formative concept phase to the design phase of a building is an ontological journey. The architect making the

fig. 20

Jacobo Mingorance Arranz's desk in Steven Holl Architects, with drawings for the Oceanic Pavilion, ChinPaoSan Necropolis, Taiwan, 2018. Photograph by Jacobo Mingorance Arranz, courtesy of Steven Holl Architects.

fig. 21

Steven Holl, Little Tesseract, Rhinebeck, New York, 2017. Photograph courtesy of Nina Stritzler-Levine.

fig. 22

Steven Holl, Watercolor Hut, Rhinebeck, New York, 2017. Courtesy of Steven Holl Architects.

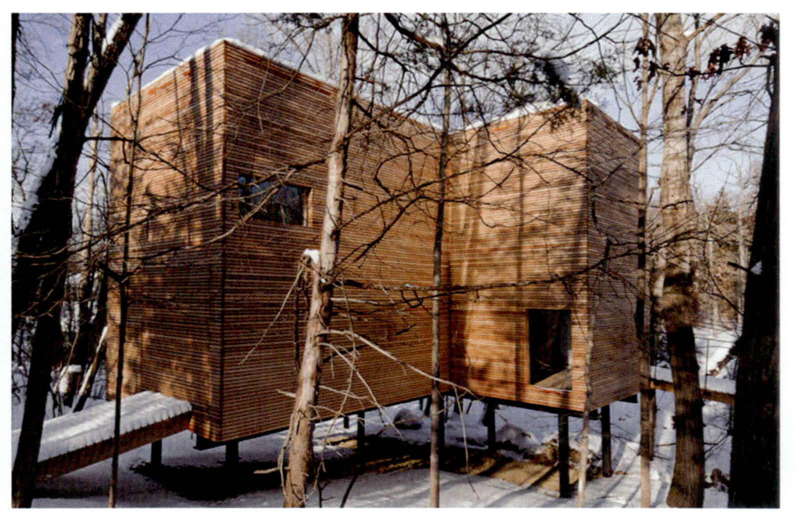

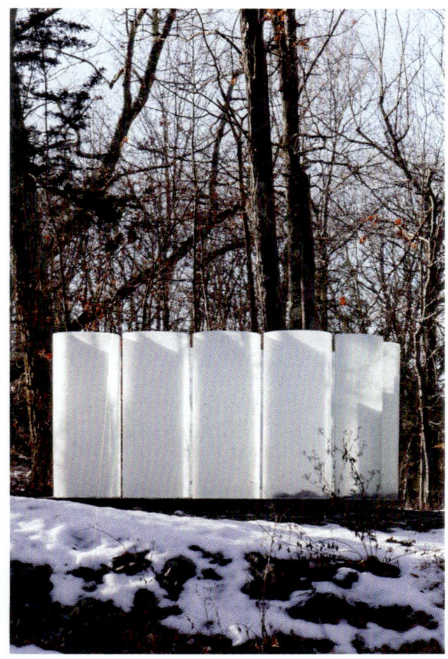

computer renderings must comprehend and then execute what Holl wants the specific representation in the watercolor to eventually become as architecture. This is the moment of transference of meaning, mood, and the soul of the phenomenal space envisioned in the watercolor.[22]

A related transference of an artistic practice into architecture happens at Holl's atelier in Rhinebeck. This is an utterly private place that is conducive to the hermetic act of drawing. Holl actually has two ateliers on his Rhinebeck property. The one on the second floor of his house has a large window, as in the New York City atelier, but here the view is of Round Lake (fig. 21). The other atelier, which he calls the Watercolor Hut, is closer to the lake (fig. 22). I imagine the making of architecture in this lakeside space becomes a world of sensory experience unto itself. This is where Holl might well imagine the feel, smell, even taste of architecture, and see it clearly in his mind, while a thicket of trees surrounds him and the light glistens off the lake. This atelier is a representation—the dramaturgy—of Holl's stated aim. The Rhinebeck property is also a laboratory, an incubator for new ideas. Holl designed each of the structures on the property: his home-atelier, the Watercolor Hut, and the T-Space Gallery (fig. 23) next to the house that hosts exhibitions of contemporary art.[23] Holl has turned the Rhinebeck property into an outdoor theater and cultural center.

The site features other experiments in three-dimensional space as well, such as the sculpture Holl conceived, had made, and then installed on the property (fig. 24). These works that he began creating in 2012

fig. 23

Steven Holl Architects, T-Space Gallery, Rhinebeck, New York. Photograph by Susan Wides, courtesy of Steven Holl Architects.

fig. 24

Steven Holl, Cold Jacket, Rhinebeck, New York. Photograph courtesy of Susan Wides.

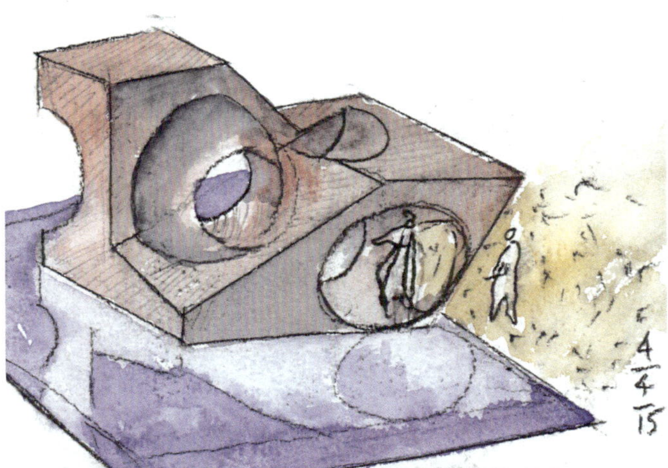

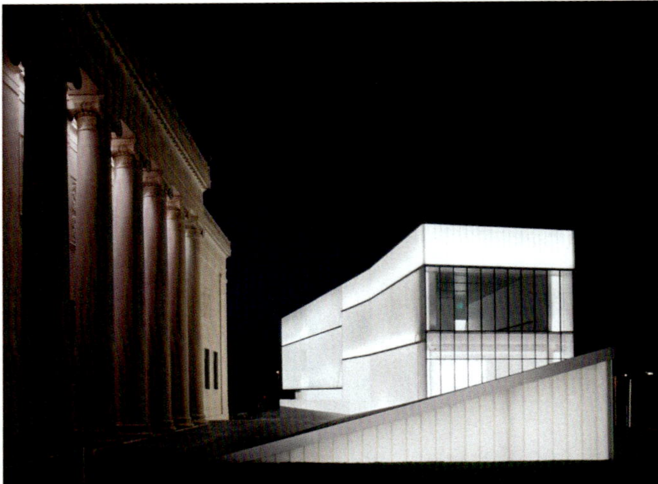

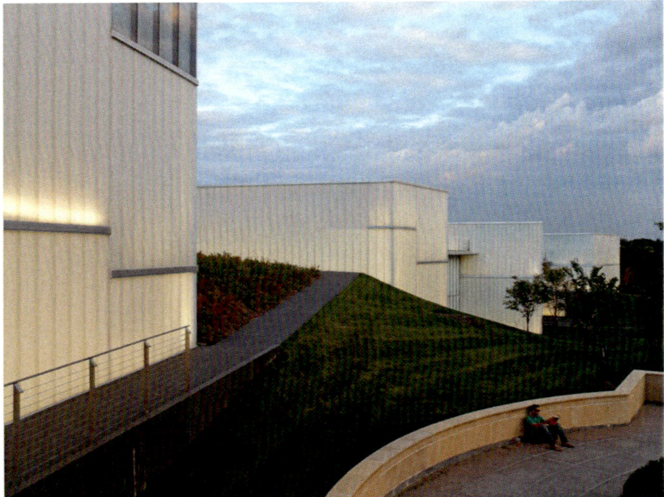

are exceptional in that they never complete the journey from abstract concept phase to the design phase that happens in Holl's architectural work. Holl draws the forms, but has the sculpture executed elsewhere, so the drawing is also critical to this practice.

Sculpture is also a transference point in the creation of architecture, as can be seen in the Ex of IN House, an experimental guesthouse Holl designed in collaboration with Tsachrelia on land across the street from the main house, which they purchased to protect the thirty acres around the main property from commercial development. In the New York City office, architects are at work on the transference of thought represented in Holl's drawings to computer renderings and models. The Ex of IN House came from the transference of ideas expressed in drawings to sculpture, and from sculpture specifically to architecture in the landscape (fig. 25). Holl began thinking about architecture as sculpture in the landscape in 1999 while working on the extension to the Nelson-Atkins Museum of Art in Kansas City, Missouri. He won that competition in a highly experimental and rather daring manner by deviating from the program that called for an addition that would physically connect a new wing to the original building. Instead, Holl conceived of the project as "a new paradigm fusing landscape and architecture." The new spaces were designed as glass lenses "scattered about the landscape of the sculpture garden" (figs. 26 and 27). Holl wanted the visitor's experience to be

fig. 25

Steven Holl, *Ex of IN Study*, 2015, watercolor on paper. Courtesy of Steven Holl Architects.

fig. 26

Steven Holl Architects, Extension, Nelson-Atkins Museum of Art, Kansas City, Kansas. Photograph by Andy Ryan, courtesy of Steven Holl Architects.

fig. 27

Steven Holl Architects, Extension, Nelson-Atkins Museum of Art, Kansas City, Kansas. Photograph by Andy Ryan, courtesy of Steven Holl Architects.

"newly charged with an experience of views and partial views of landscape." He created "sequences of shifting perspectives . . . spaces where landscape merges with architecture."[24] Holl drew this sequence diagrammatically as landscape-art-architecture in two intertwining dashed lines. When he published the diagram shortly after, in the book *Parallax*, he compared it to a different and now well-known diagram showing connections between sculpture, landscape, and architecture from Rosalind Krauss's canonical essay "Sculpture in the Expanded Field" (fig. 28).[25] With the evocative juxtaposition of these diagrams Holl seemed to be suggesting that, like Krauss, he was redefining the relationships between architecture, sculpture, and landscape, and redefining architecture as a sculptural practice.

The making of the Ex of IN House is further evidence of this redefining. The house is a completed "abstract journey" of an idea as it emerged initially in sculptural form. Holl and Tsachrelia called the series of sculptures that led to the creation of the house *Explorations of IN* (fig. 29). Unlike the abstract sculpture on the Rhinebeck property, the *Explorations of IN* reached a state of being real. In other words, they eventually became architecture. The interplay of open geometric volumes in the interiors of the house is a conceptual transference from the *Explorations of IN* studies to architecture (fig. 30). The house connects to the landscape through the expansive fenestration (fig. 31). On one

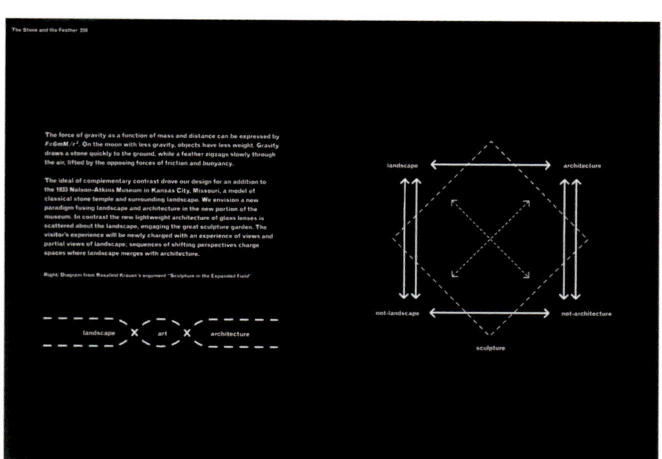

The Stone and the Feather 256

The force of gravity as a function of mass and distance can be expressed by $F=GmM/r^2$. On the moon with less gravity, objects have less weight. Gravity draws a stone quickly to the ground, while a feather zigzags slowly through the air, lifted by the opposing forces of friction and buoyancy.

The ideal of complementary contrast drove our design for an addition to the 1933 Nelson-Atkins Museum in Kansas City, Missouri, a model of classical stone temple and surrounding landscape. We envision a new paradigm fusing landscape and architecture in the new portion of the museum. In contrast the new lightweight architecture of glass lenses is scattered about the landscape, engaging the great sculpture garden. The visitor's experience will be newly charged with an experience of views and partial views of landscape; sequences of shifting perspectives charge spaces where landscape merges with architecture.

Right: Diagram from Rosalind Krauss's argument "Sculpture in the Expanded Field"

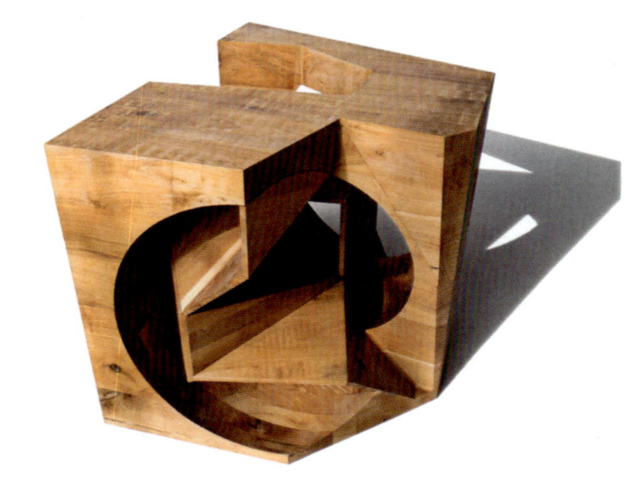

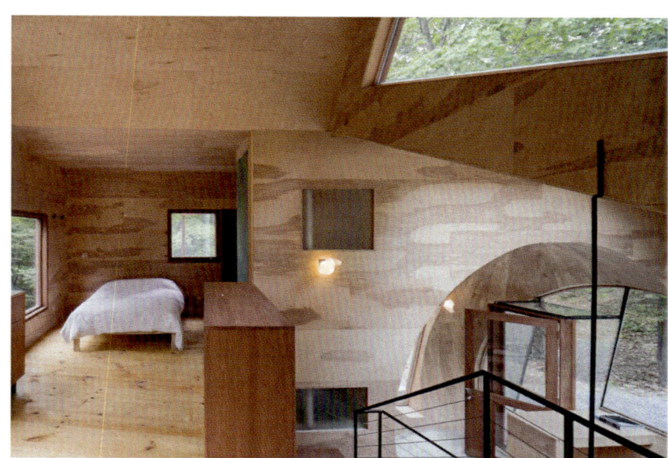

fig. 28

Steven Holl, *Concept Diagram for the Nelson-Atkins Museum of Art*, Kansas City, Kansas, and Steven Holl, *Diagram for "logically expanded field,"* from Rosalind Krauss, "Sculpture in the Expanded Field," republished in Steven Holl, *Parallax*, 256–57.

fig. 29

Steven Holl Architects, *Exploration of IN*, 2015, CNC-milled walnut. Courtesy of Steven Holl Architects.

fig. 30

Steven Holl Architects, Ex of IN House, interior, Rhinebeck, New York, 2016. Courtesy of Steven Holl Architects.

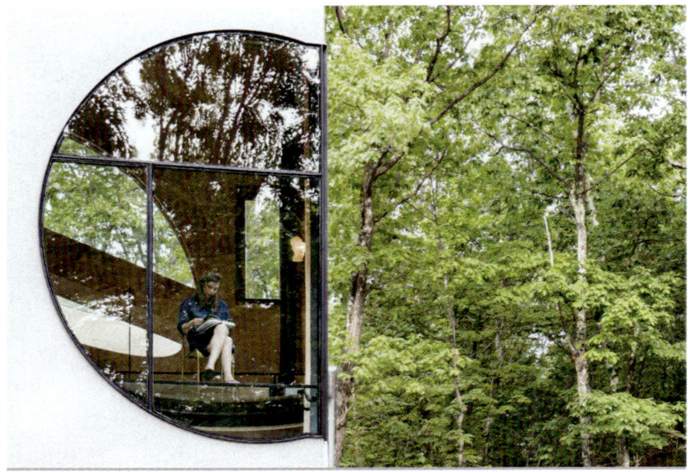

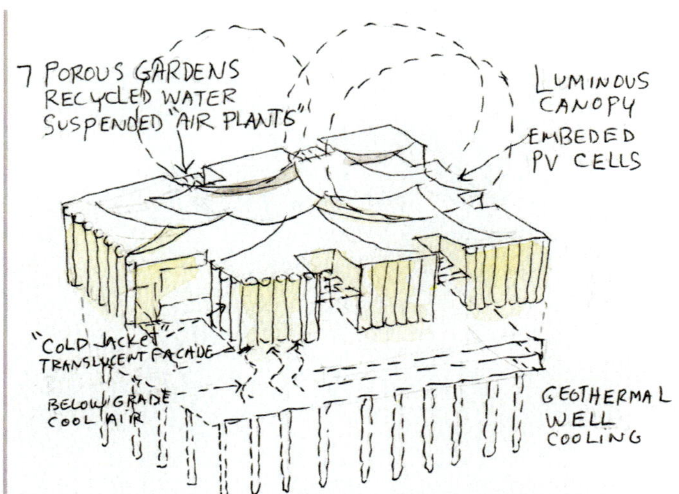

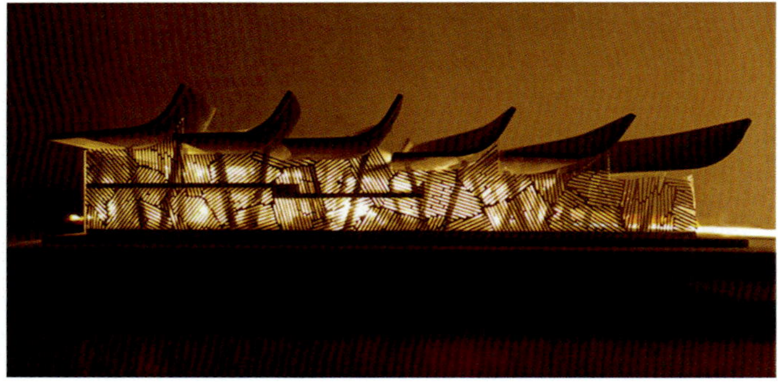

side that looks out to the dense forest, Holl and Tsachrelia installed glass on the floor in front of the window to heighten the reflective qualities of the light and to bring the nature more vividly into the house.

The light effects that Holl and Tsachrelia showed to be critical in the creation of space with "strong phenomenal properties" in the Ex of IN House appear in different dimensions across the diverse projects that constitute Holl's current body of work. In Rhinebeck the space and light were sculpted; in the expansion to Museum of Fine Arts, Houston, light penetrates the interiors through the roof conceived as a luminous canopy (fig. 32). Light resonates in the interiors of the Malawi Library and in the Rubenstein Commons at the Institute for Advanced Studies in Princeton through what Holl calls "the billowing roof" (figs. 33 and 34).

BODY IN MOTION

Further elaboration on the conceptual transference from sculpture to architecture to landscape is evident in the extension to the Kennedy Center for the Performing Arts in Washington, DC, that Holl conceived as three white concrete pavilions (figs. 35 and 36). The pavilions, whose materiality and particular positioning in the landscape is similar to the paradigm Holl created for the Nelson-Atkins Museum, are best understood as a sculptural formation when compared to *Shift* (fig. 37), one of the most acclaimed works by Richard Serra. Composed of six

fig. 31

Steven Holl Architects, Ex of IN House, interior and surrounding landscape, Rhinebeck, New York, 2016. Courtesy of Steven Holl Architects.

fig. 32

Steven Holl, *Luminous Canopy*, Museum of Fine Arts, Houston, Texas, 2012, watercolor on paper. Courtesy of Steven Holl Architects.

fig. 33

Steven Holl Architects, *Sectional Presentation Model*, Malawi Library, Lilongwe, Malawi, 2017, resin-impregnated plaster 3D print and laser-cut paper, CNC-milled plywood, and acrylic base. Courtesy of Steven Holl Architects.

massive concrete volumes, *Shift* extends out in a zigzag formation embedded in what was a vast swath of open land in King City, Canada, when Serra installed it between 1970 and 1972. As Rosalind Krauss has explained, the specific positioning of *Shift* in the landscape was informed by the phenomenological thought of the French philosopher Maurice Merleau-Ponty (a favorite of Holl's).[26] The manner in which Serra rigorously laid out the six concrete volumes of *Shift* in the landscape derived from the phenomenological notion that sensory experiences are enhanced as the body moves through space. Serra created an experience between the sculpture and the site in the landscape that required the body to be in motion to bring it fully into view. The configuration of the three cement volumes of the Kennedy Center expansion echoes the zigzag formation of *Shift*, aiming as well to enhance the sensory experience as the body moves around and through the architecture and the surrounding landscape.

Holl returned to drawing a diagram with intertwined dashed lines as he had done for the Nelson-Atkins Museum, again evoking the body in motion in several of his practice's current projects. The concept diagram for Rubenstein Commons at the Institute for Advanced Study, called INTERTWINING, ENMESHING, literally expresses his enduring aim to create space with "strong phenomenal properties" (fig. 38). The melding of words and images that surround the floor plan at the center of the drawing expresses the

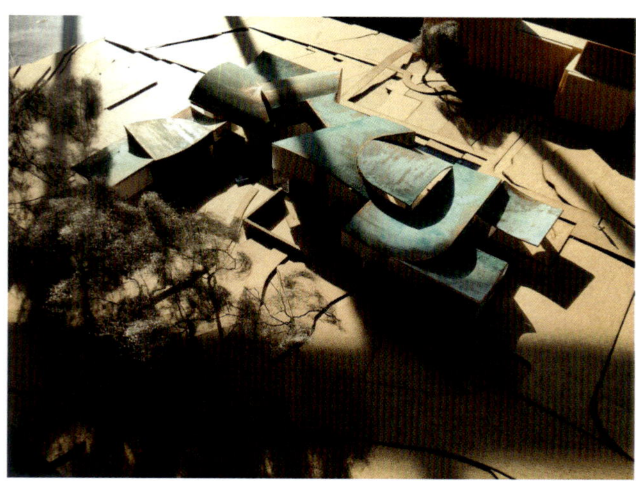

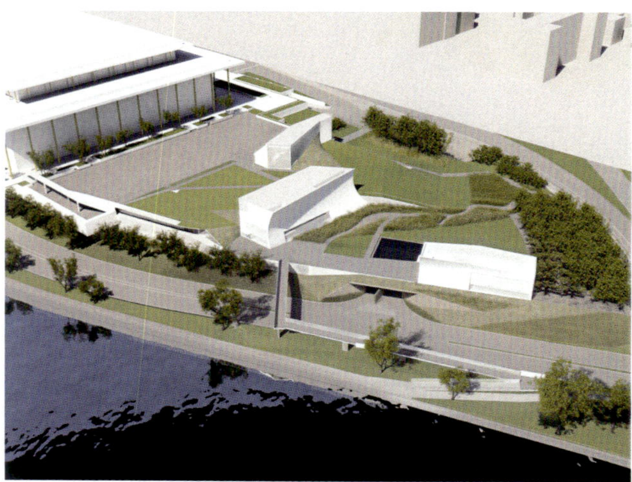

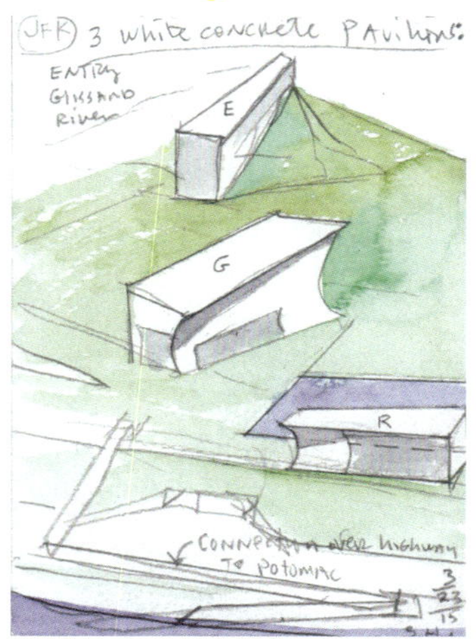

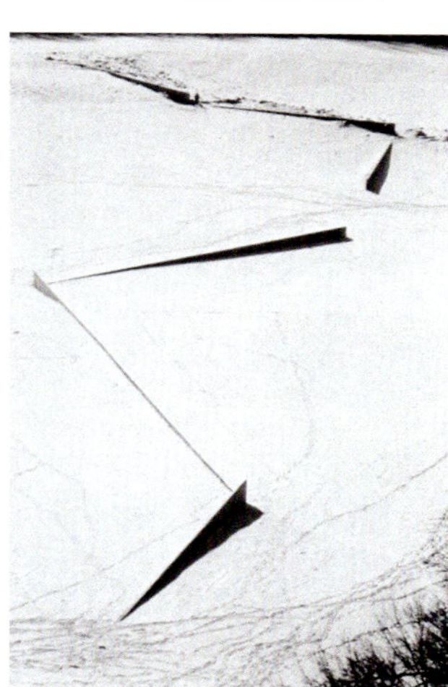

fig. 34

Steven Holl Architects, *Presentation Model*, Rubenstein Commons, Institute for Advanced Studies, Princeton, New Jersey, 2017, resin-impregnated plaster 3D print, copper patina paint. Courtesy of Steven Holl Architects.

fig. 35

Steven Holl Architects, *Schematic Design Study Model*, John F. Kennedy Center for the Performing Arts Expansion, Washington, DC, 2013, resin-impregnated plaster 3D prints on chipboard, acrylic base. Courtesy of Steven Holl Architects.

fig. 36

Steven Holl, *3 White Concrete Pavilions*, John F. Kennedy Center for the Performing Arts Expansion, Washington, DC, 2012, watercolor on paper. Courtesy of Steven Holl Architects.

fig. 37

Richard Serra, *Shift*, 1970–72, six concrete sections, King City, Canada. © 2018 Richard Serra / Artists Rights Society (ARS), New York.

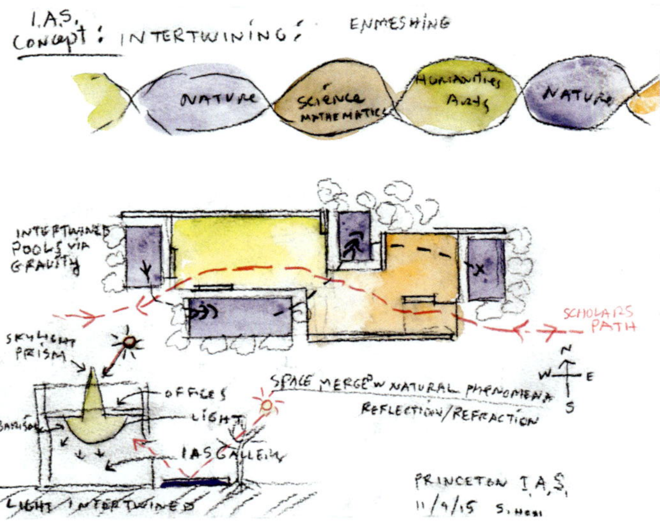

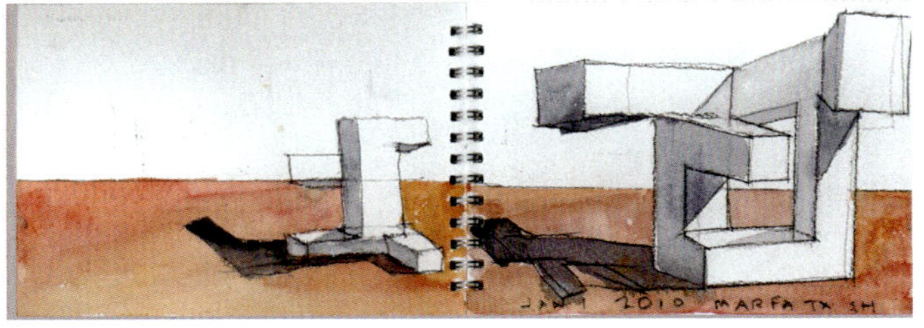

core idea; the orchestrated architectural conditions and elements will create a merging of space with natural phenomena. Walking along the "scholars path," as Holl called it, and represented here as intertwined dashed lines, is a representation of the body moving through the interior spaces as it will encounter views from the windows looking out to pools of water and the landscape beyond. Holl also depicted the institutional mission of the institute—connecting science, mathematics, humanities, and arts—in the intertwining lines of the diagram at the top of the same drawing. The word "nature" written on a background wash of blue is the same color as the intertwined pools of water on the floor plan, where the interconnected experiences of the body in motion and the flow of knowledge across the disciplines are expressed.

While the buildings underway in the former Hudson Rail Yards, mentioned earlier, are creating a new skyline on Manhattan's West Side, Holl's focus is elsewhere in New York City.[27] Across the East River in the borough of Queens on one of the most visually arresting sites in New York City, the Hunters Point Community Library, Holl's largest and most complex building in the city, is under construction. The emphatic horizontality of the design stands out along the river and against the tall buildings behind it (fig. 39). The pronounced sculptural form of the library bears comparison with minimalist sculpture by Donald Judd that Holl made a subject of

fig. 38

Steven Holl, *Space Merged w/ Natural Phenomena*, Rubenstein Commons, Institute for Advanced Studies, Princeton, New Jersey, 2015, watercolor on paper. Courtesy of Steven Holl Architects.

fig. 39

Steven Holl Architects, Hunters Point Community Library, New York, 2017. Courtesy of Steven Holl Architects.

fig. 40

Steven Holl, *Marfa*, TX, 2010, watercolor on paper. Courtesy of Steven Holl Architects.

his drawings when he visited Judd's home and studio in Marfa, Texas (fig. 40). As a *chantier* (the French word for a building in the emergent state of becoming architecture), the interpenetration of interior and exterior space is awe inspiring (fig. 41). Here Holl aims to make space with phenomenal properties by cutting into the exterior walls at various angles and in pronounced shapes.

Over the years, Holl has made watercolors of such cuts, creating what he calls "subtractive space" (fig. 42). These openings redefine the window as a basic architectural element. From a single vantage point through the cut in the east wall of the Hunters Point Community Library, the views of Manhattan across the river encompass the Chrysler Building, the Empire State Building, and the United Nations. Here as in ChinPaoSan Necropolis in Taiwan and the Institute for Contemporary Art at Virginia Commonwealth University, the positioning of architectural elements, particularly stairs and ramps, reveals yet another way Holl orchestrates interior space to heighten sensory experience (figs. 43 and 44)—especially by positioning them close to the windows in these projects. Holl has made study drawings of such architectural elements that recall the haunting images of Piranesi (fig. 45). To understand the potential feeling of these embodied spaces, think about what it is like to be on one of the many escalators that today move people through public buildings. This is how the architect

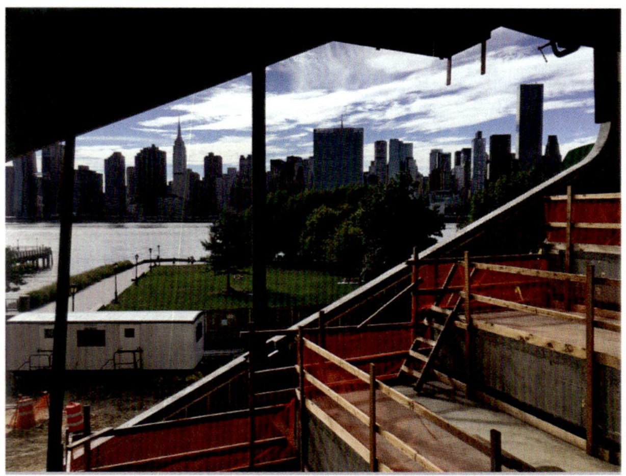

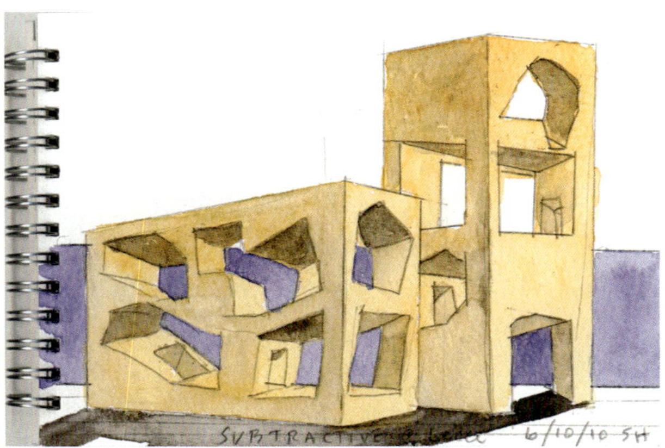

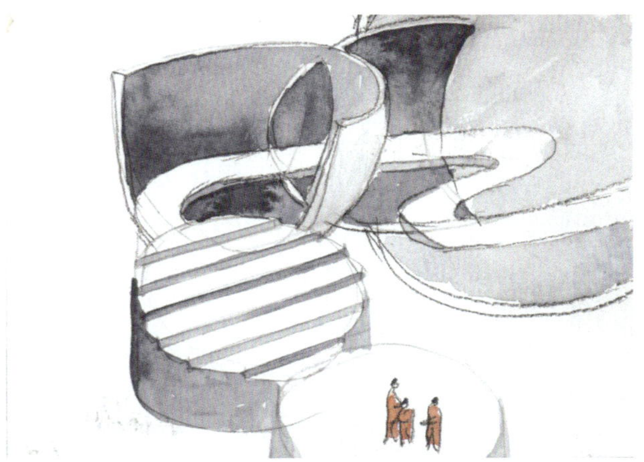

fig. 41

Steven Holl Architects, Hunters Point Community Library, New York, 2017. Courtesy of Steven Holl Architects.

fig. 42

Steven Holl, *Subtractive*, 2010, watercolor on paper. Courtesy of Steven Holl Architects.

fig. 43

Steven Holl, *Oceanic Journey*, ChinPaoSan, Necropolis, Taiwan, 2014, watercolor on paper. Courtesy of Steven Holl Architects.

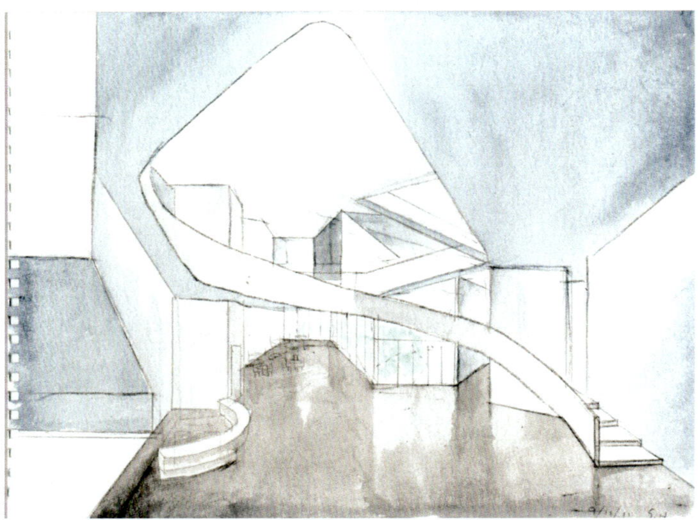

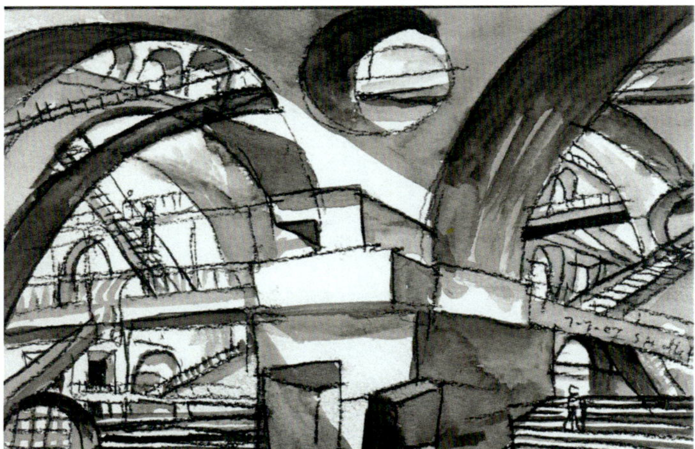

determined the kind of experience the body in motion would have in museums like MoMA, for example, or in Frank Gehry's recently completed Fondation Louis Vuitton in Paris. While a practical choice, the escalator that moves people through narrow channels of dark space stifles the senses rather than stimulating them. By instead positioning stairs along windows with penetrating light, and ramps with sweeping curves across monumental interiors, Holl seeks to enhance synaptic connections—those that move the body willed by the mind through physical space.

Holl's enduring aim brings to mind John Rajchman's explanation of how the French philosopher Gilles Deleuze sought to question the meaning of philosophy in contemporary life. Deleuze found "new ways of connecting philosophy and connecting with philosophy."[28] As the architect-artist, Holl pursues such lines of connectivity between philosophy and architecture as a form of resistance against the mundane commercialization of contemporary architecture, and as a means of enlivening architecture to enrich everyday life.

fig. 44

Steven Holl, *Forum*, Institute of Contemporary Art, Virginia Commonwealth University, Richmond, 2011, watercolor on paper. Courtesy of Steven Holl Architects.

fig. 45

Steven Holl, *Interior with Stairs, after Piranesi*, July 2007, watercolor on paper. Courtesy of Steven Holl Architects.

NOTES

Epigraph: Steven Holl, "Intertwining," in *Intertwining: Steven Holl, Selected Projects 1989–1995* (New York: Princeton Architectural Press, 1996), 16.

1. Alberto Pérez-Gómez, "Translation vs. Transcription," *Architectural Representation and the Perspective Hinge*, Alberto Pérez-Gómez and Louise Pelletier (Cambridge, MA: MIT Press, 1997), 3.
2. Steven Holl, "Scale," Steven Holl—Scale: An Artist's Sketchbook, ed. Lars Müller (Zurich: Lars Müller, 2012), n.p.
3. Quoted from Keith Albarn and Jenny Miall Smith, *Diagram: The Instrument of Thought* (London: Thames and Hudson, 1977), in "Thinking Through Diagrams: In Search of True Architectural Autonomy," Matías Imbern (paper for Does Architecture Exist?, MIT, n.d.), www.igc-ar.com/paper/121212_Thinking%20Through%20Diagrams.pdf.
4. To my knowledge these diagrams have not been previously published.
5. Among the most prominent of this broad representation of architects are Rem Koolhaas, Bernard Tschumi, Jacques Herzog, and Pierre de Meuron. Quoted from Anthony Vidler, "Diagrams of Diagrams: Architectural Abstraction and Modern Representation," *Representations* 72 (Autumn 2002): 2.
6. Frank Gehry draws by hand using ink and paper in a process that Horst Bredekamp has explained is "intertwined with every planning stage" of a project. See Horst Bredekamp, "Frank Gehry and the Art of Drawing," in *Gehry Draws*, ed. Mark Rappolt and Robert Violette (Cambridge, MA: MIT Press in association with Violette Editions, London, 2004), 13.
7. Holl discussed these ideas when he spoke at the Salk Institute in 2017. The lecture is expected to be available on the Steven Holl Architects website. For discussions of neuroscience and architecture, see Sarah Robinson and Juhani Pallasmaa, eds., *Mind in Architecture: Neuroscience, Embodiment, and the Future of Design* (Cambridge, MA: MIT Press, 2015).
8. See the monograph Robert McCarter, *Steven Holl* (London: Phaidon, 2015).
9. For an analysis of this project through the lens of Merleau-Pontian phenomenology, see Scott Drake, "The 'Chiasm' and the Experience of Space: Steven Holl's Museum of Contemporary Art, Helsinki," *Journal of Architectural Education* 59, no. 2 (November 2005): 53–59.
10. Lebbeus Woods, "Foreword," in *Steven Holl Architecture Spoken* (New York: Rizzoli, 2007).
11. Two volumes, *Pamphlet Architecture 1–10* and *11–20*, reprint the journal's first twenty issues, originally published individually between 1978 and 2002 (New York: Princeton Architectural Press, 1998 and 2011), 6.
12. The syllabus had a lengthy list of architect-artists: El Lissitzky, Frederick Kiesler, and Luis Barragan among them. While working on this project I attended several of Holl's classes. He is an accessible and deeply engaged teacher who encourages his students to draw by hand, to think about architecture as an interdisciplinary practice, and to develop knowledge of architectural history. In spring 2017 Holl and Dimitra Tsachrelia co-taught an advanced studio class in the Columbia University Graduate School of Architecture, Planning and Preservation called Architectonics of Music: Time-Scale, which explored how the rhythm, counterpoint, and scale that guide the creation of music can also inform the creation of interior space. The seminar in fall 2017 examined architects who worked with painters and sculptors or were themselves practicing these and other art disciplines. Holl sees his work as part of this historical trajectory. He revealed this heritage in the book *Urban Hopes*, which positions his recent work in China in relation to major urban projects of the twentieth century, such as Karl-Marx-Hof in Vienna and Rockefeller Center in New York, along with visionary projects by El Lissitzky, Buckminster Fuller, Yona Friedman, Archigram, and others. See Christoph a. Kumpusch, ed., *Urban Hopes: Made in China by Steven Holl* (Zurich: Lars Müller, 2014).
13. *Emilio Ambasz / Steven Holl: Architecture*, February 9–April 4, 1989. See https://www.moma.org/calendar/exhibitions/1774?locale=en for information on this project. Emilio Ambasz is the visionary former design curator at MoMA who had been working as an architect since his departure from the museum several years before.
14. Paul Goldberger, "ARCHITECTURE VIEW: Two Architects Who Tap Into Our Deepest Moods," *New York Times*, February 12, 1989, http://www.nytimes.com/1989/02/12/arts/architecture-view-two-architects-who-tap-into-our-deepest-moods.
15. After working for a decade in various places across

Asia, Steven Holl Architects opened an office in Beijing, China, in 2006, a clear sign it had become a worldwide practice. See McCarter, *Steven Holl*, and Kumpusch, *Urban Hopes*.

16. Phone interview with the author, May 2017. Piggott told me she had been involved in many projects, but the one with the Holl office was exceptional. She explained they had a way of presenting their ideas and helping a layperson. She admired how the architects were constantly evaluating the program.
17. Other such micro-aims appear in the Projects section of this volume.
18. On the idea of the architect-artist, see Le Corbusier, *New World of Space: Le Corbusier, the Foundations of His Work* (New York: Reynal & Hitchcock, 1948). The publication was the catalogue to an exhibition of the same name at the Institute of Contemporary Art, Boston, one of the few in the United States on Le Corbusier up until this time that considered his paintings. The catalogue includes a text by Le Corbusier in which he elaborates on the architect-artist.
19. This is one of the most trafficked thoroughfares in New York City, connecting Manhattan to Weehawken, New Jersey.
20. With the Port Authority bus station several blocks to the north at 42nd Street, and the Pennsylvania Railroad station just two blocks to the east at 34th Street, many of the passersby are likely heading to one of those transit hubs. Others are perhaps searching for the entrance to the High Line, the elevated pedestrian walkway, which is partially obscured beneath the scaffolds of the adjacent construction site.
21. Here again it is worth noting the comparison to Le Corbusier, the most revered architect-artist. Le Corbusier had an office in the center of Paris, called atelier rue de Sèvres, and ateliers in more secluded locations, including one in his home (which, when he moved there in the 1930s, was on the outskirts of Paris) and another in Cap Martin, a remote area on the coast of the Mediterranean. On this point, see Jean-Louis Cohen, *Le Corbusier La planète comme chantier* (Paris: Les Éditions Textuel, 2015).
22. Holl explained this idea in "Abstract Journey," in *Parallax* (New York: Princeton Architectural Press, 2000), 345–46; and, more recently, in "What is Architecture?," *Brooklyn Rail*, September 4, 2013, https://brooklynrail.org/2013/09/criticspage/what-is-architecture-art. I want to thank Jacobo Mingorance Arranz for giving me access to his desk in the Holl office.
23. The Steven Myron Holl Foundation, a non-profit organization, coordinates all of the activities and sponsors the summer fellowship program for architects at the Rhinebeck property.
24. Holl, *Parallax*, 256.
25. Rosalind Krauss, "Sculpture in the Expanded Field," in *The Originality of the Avant-Garde and Other Modernist Myths*, ed. Rosalind Krauss (Cambridge, MA: MIT Press, 1991), 276–90. There is some confusion in how the diagram from the Krauss text is depicted in *Parallax*. The caption in *Parallax* identifies the drawing as "Diagram from Rosalind Krauss's argument 'Sculpture in the Expanded Field.'" Of the three diagrams illustrated in Krauss's essay, it is closest to the one on page 283, but the version Holl published is incomplete. It is missing the question marks at the top and two side points of the diamond, and is missing the word "complex" that extends from "architecture," as well as the word "neuter" that extends from "not-architecture." Krauss's argument centered on defining a new nomenclature for sculpture: earthworks, for example, were called sculpture but were not sculpture per se. She considered how Robert Smithson's *Spiral Jetty* is embedded in the landscape, or how *Perimeters/Pavilions/Decoys* by Mary Miss is constructed—its form, and the structural expanse. Comparing Holl's visionary work Parallax Towers with Miss's *Perimeters/Pavilions/Decoys* demonstrates the ambiguity in determining what is architecture and what is sculpture, for Holl's work appears to be an inverted version of Miss's piece. Holl's argument about the relationships between landscape, architecture, and sculpture in the Nelson-Atkins Museum expansion project was foremost asserting the merging of architecture and landscape through the intermediating conjoining of art that appears in the center of Holl's diagram.
26. Rosalind Krauss, "Richard Serra, a Translation," in *The Originality of the Avant-Garde*, 260–74. In particular, Krauss referred to the impact of Merleau-Ponty's *Phenomenology of Perception* on Serra. For the importance of that book on Holl, see Kenneth Frampton, *Steven Holl: Architect* (Milan: Electa Architecture, 2003).
27. Holl was among the first to contemplate the future of the Hudson Rail Yards in the visionary project "Edge of a City," which he first published in issue 13 of *Pamphlet Architecture* in 1991.
28. John Rajchman, *The Deleuzian Connections* (Cambridge, MA: MIT Press, 2000), 4–5.

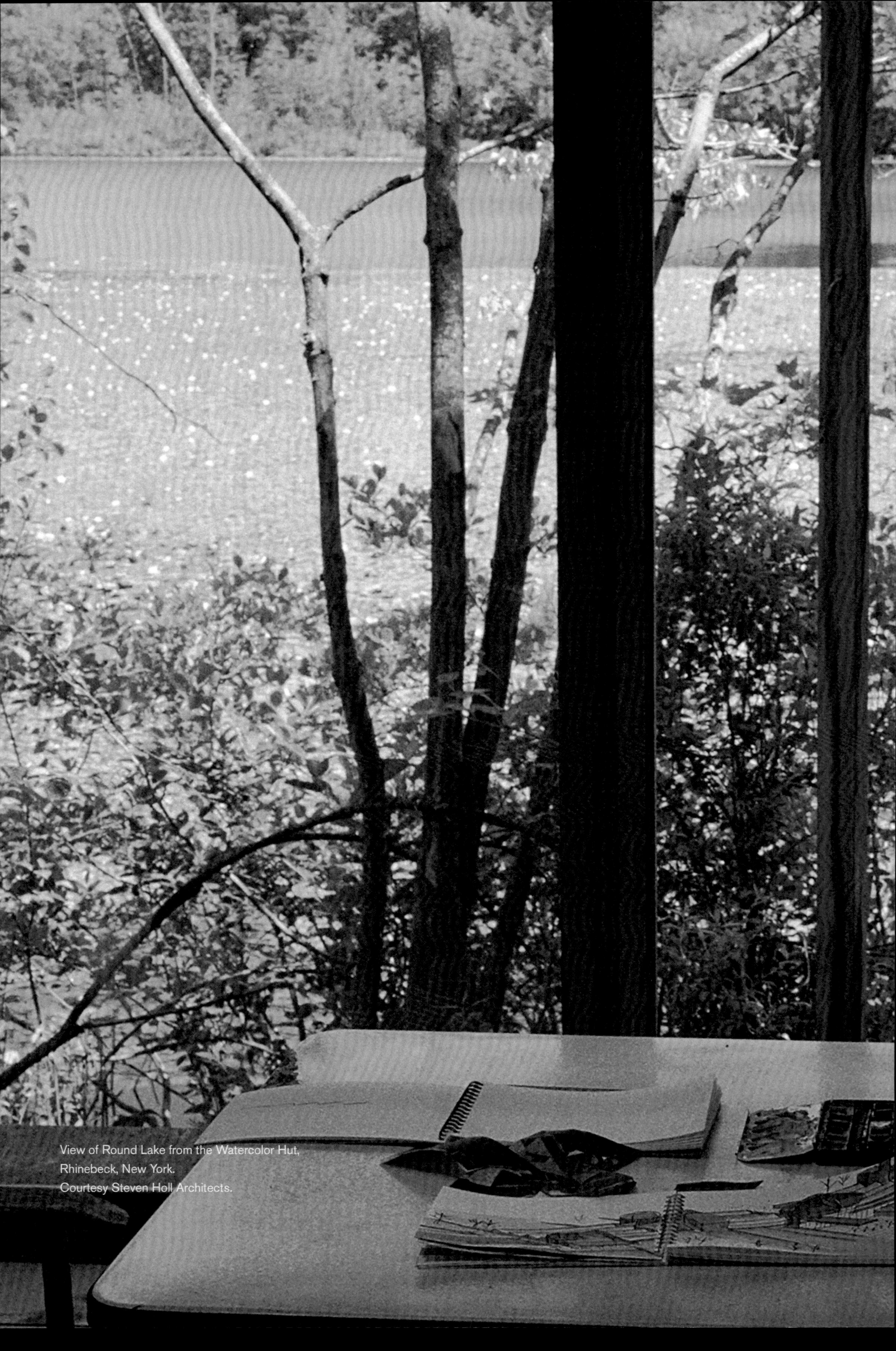

View of Round Lake from the Watercolor Hut,
Rhinebeck, New York.
Courtesy Steven Holl Architects.

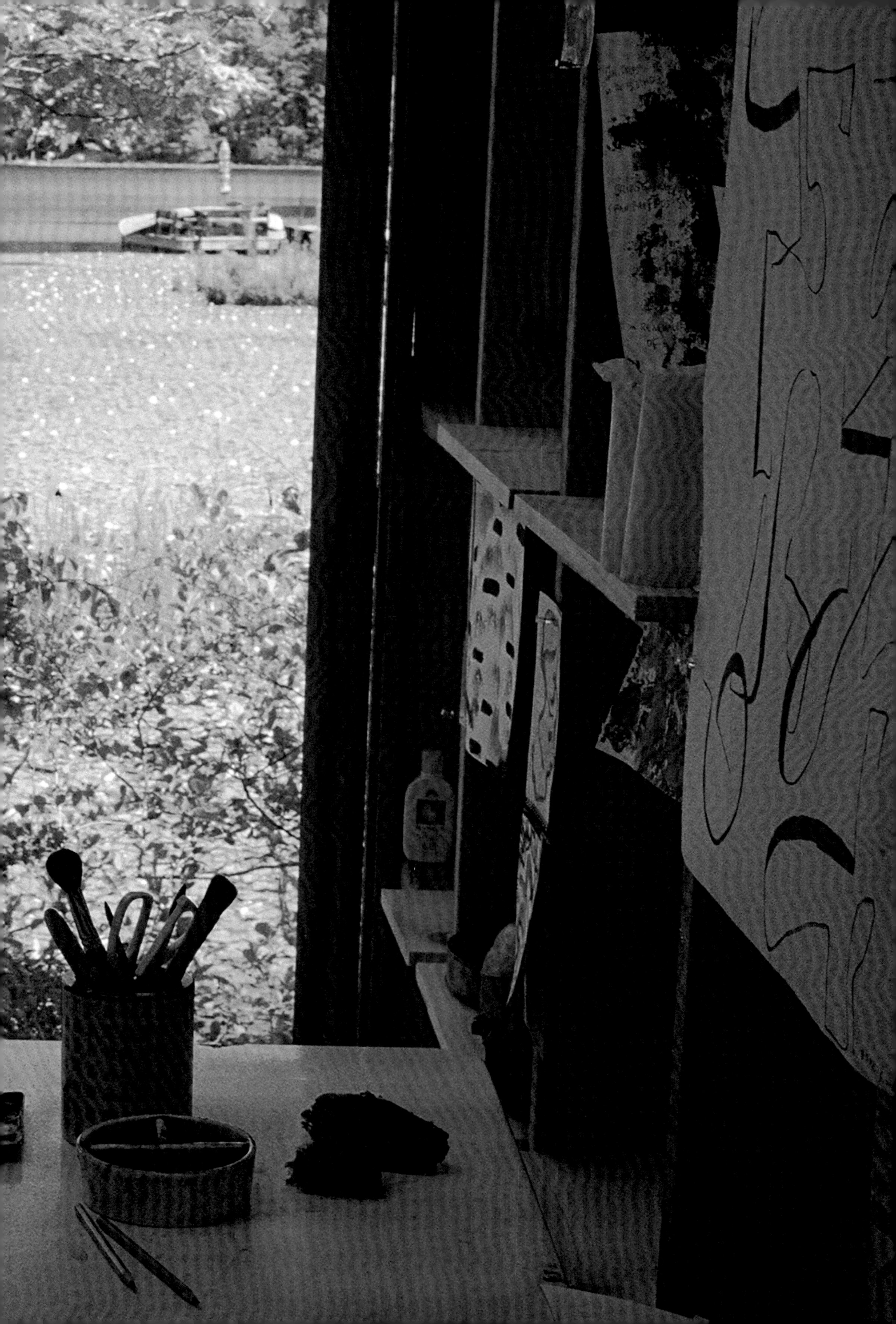

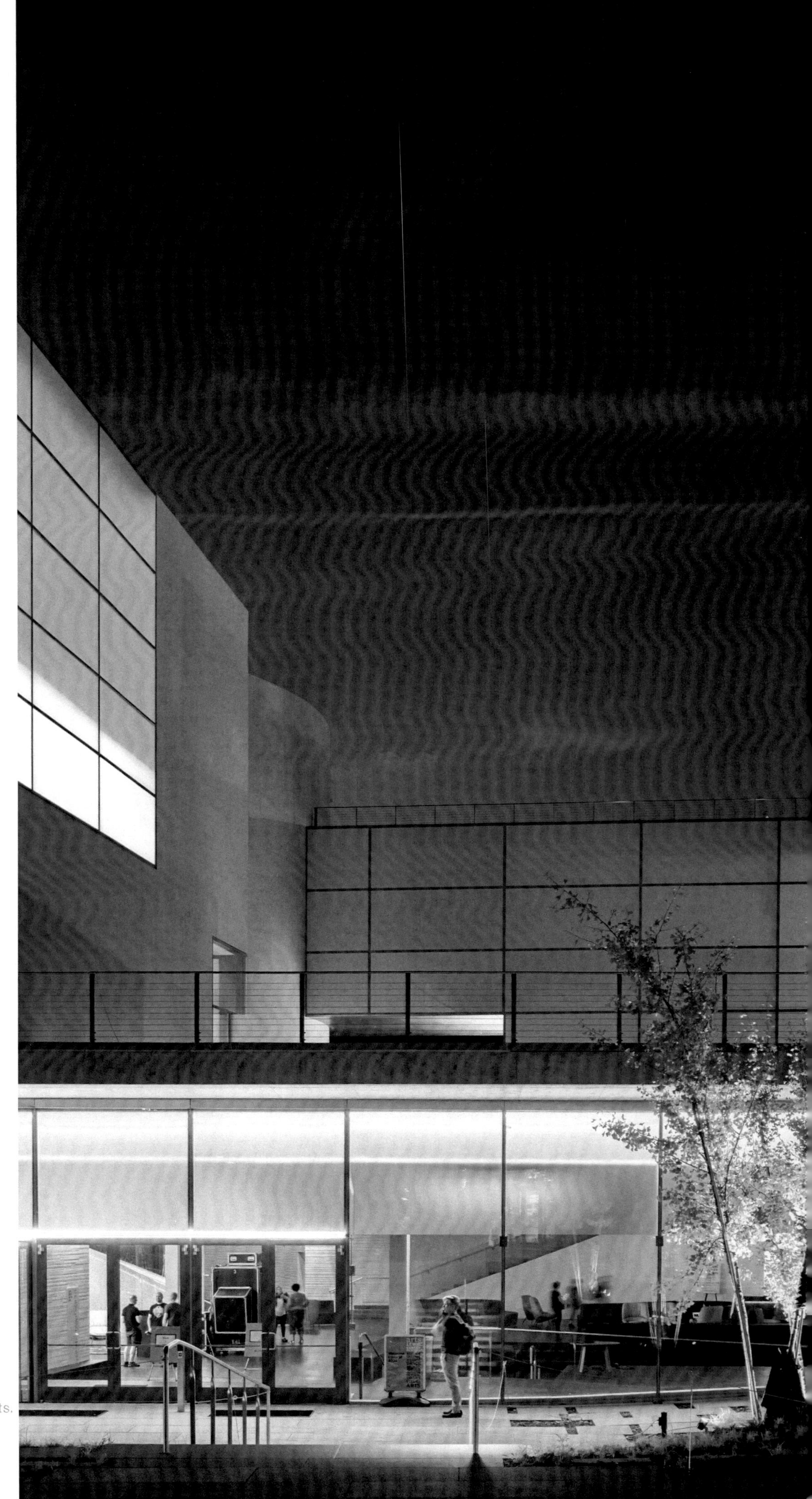

Steven Holl Architects,
Lewis Center for the Arts, Princeton University, model.
Courtesy Steven Holl Architects.

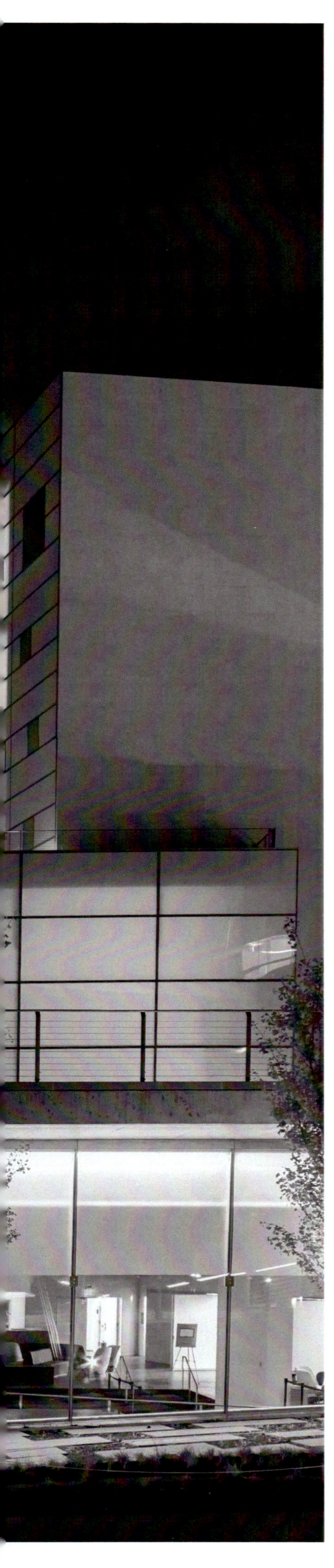

IN UNION WITH THE LAND: HUDSON VALLEY TRADITIONS AND STEVEN HOLL'S ARCHITECTURE

Kerry Dean Carso

Thomas Cole's "Essay on American Scenery" (1836) ruminates on the unique splendor of nature in the nineteenth-century United States. The founder of the Hudson River School of landscape painting, Cole valued untouched scenery, and he declared that "the Hudson for natural magnificence is unsurpassed" (fig. 46).[1] Cole lived in Catskill, New York; in nearby Rhinebeck, Steven Holl has a home and studio. Although Holl's architectural firm is in New York City, and he has enjoyed commissions all over the world, his buildings share important concerns with art and architecture traditions in the Hudson River Valley.

In 1837 the American architect Alexander Jackson Davis published *Rural Residences*, in which he lamented that in American rural architecture, "Defects are felt . . . in the want of connexion [sic] with [a building's] site."[2] His book attempted to remedy this defect by illustrating buildings nestled within their natural settings. Davis's collaborator, Andrew Jackson Downing, concurred. A native of Newburgh, New York, Downing was a horticulturist, landscape gardener, and tastemaker who designed landscapes for elite Hudson Valley clients. In his pattern books targeted to genteel readers, Downing popularized the veranda or porch as a place of domestic social

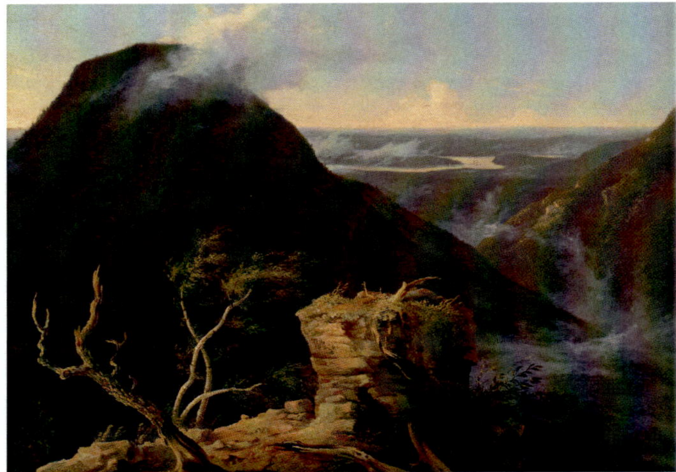

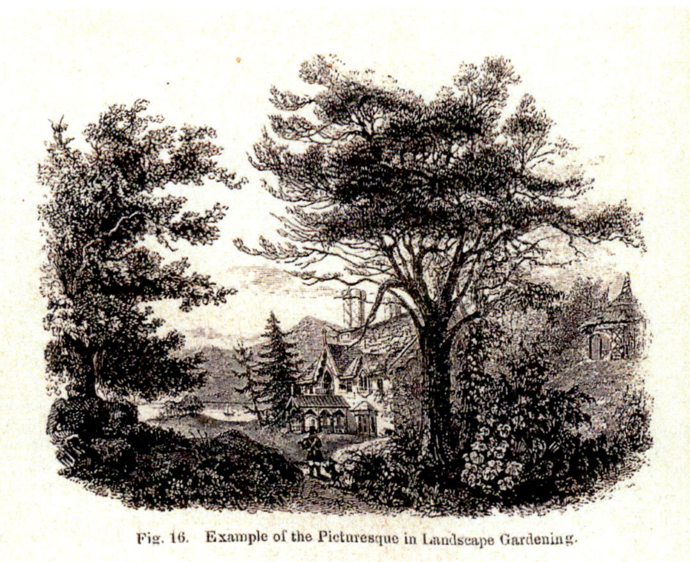

Fig. 16. Example of the Picturesque in Landscape Gardening.

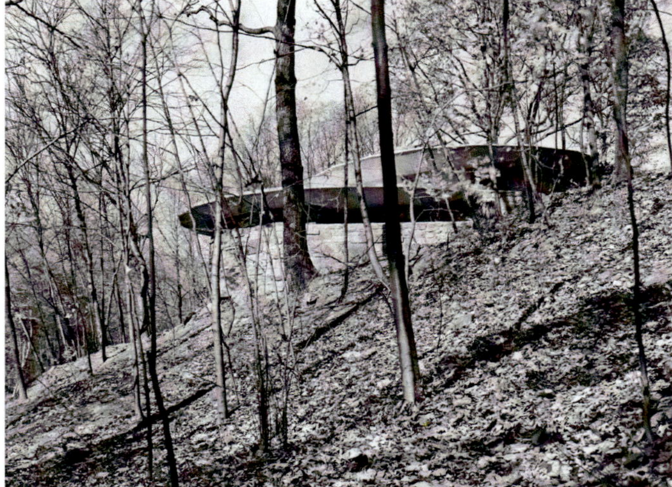

interaction; the veranda also functioned as a liminal space, connecting the house interior with the outside. Protected from the elements by the veranda's roof and yet situated outdoors with breezes and views, veranda users enjoyed access to nature, an idea at the heart of nineteenth-century American Romanticism. Advocating for picturesque profiles in domestic architecture, Downing wrote that "various projections and irregularities, caused by verandas, porticoes, etc. [serve] to connect the otherwise square masses of building, by gradual transition, with the ground about it."[3] Downing's illustration of the picturesque in landscape gardening (fig. 47) demonstrates how an irregular Gothic revival house blends into the unkempt naturalistic style of gardening that Downing advocated in his books.

The architecture of American modernist Frank Lloyd Wright emerged out of nineteenth-century Romantic theory in that he advocated site-specificity and organic architecture. Wright's Sol Friedman Residence

fig. 46

Thomas Cole, *View of the Round-Top in the Catskill Mountains*, 1827, oil on panel. Museum of Fine Arts, Boston, Gift of Martha C. Karolik for the M. and M. Karolik Collection of American Paintings, 1815–1865 (47.1200). Photograph © 2018 Museum of Fine Arts, Boston.

fig. 47

Andrew Jackson Downing, "Example of the Picturesque in Landscape Gardening," facing p. 273 in *A Treatise on the Theory and Practice of Landscape Gardening* (1841; New York: C. M. Saxton & Co., 1855). Courtesy of Sojourner Truth Library, State University of New York at New Paltz.

fig. 48

Frank Lloyd Wright, Friedman House, exterior, site view, Armonk, New York, 1948–50. Photograph © Ezra Stoller/Esto. All rights reserved.

in Pleasantville, New York (1948–50), for example, appears to grow organically from its site, blending in seamlessly with its natural environment (fig. 48). About a Usonian house like the Friedman Residence, Wright wrote, "Where does the garden leave off and the house begin? Where the garden begins and the house leaves off. Withal, this Usonian dwelling seems a thing loving the ground with the new sense of space, light and freedom—to which our USA is entitled."[4] Mid-twentieth-century architectural historians noted the debt Wright owed to nineteenth-century Romantic thought and to Downing, in particular. During Wright's lifetime, Vincent Scully noted that Wright strove "to keep alive that sense of union with the land which had been at the root of the intrinsically American domestic development since the time of Andrew Jackson Downing. . . One must conclude that in Wright's work the creative traditions of the 19th century still live and have given rise to the new."[5]

Today, Steven Holl shares this desire to create architecture in "union with the land." He uses the term "anchoring": "The site of a building is more than a mere ingredient in its conception. It is its physical and metaphysical foundation."[6] Holl exploits transparent materials to bring outside in, for instance in his Ex of IN House (2016) in Rhinebeck. Here one is surrounded by what Cole called the "favored regions," an escape from the city into a world where "land and water in the play of light and shadow yields delight." In Cole's favored regions, one drinks "from pleasure's purest cup."[7] At the Ex of IN House, the play of water ripples as shadows across surfaces tap into the primordial desire to immerse oneself in nature. The legacies of Cole, Davis, Downing, and Wright live on in Holl's conception of architecture in nature.

NOTES

1. Thomas Cole, "Essay on American Scenery," in *American Art 1700–1960: Sources and Documents*, ed. John W. McCoubrey (Englewood Cliff, NJ: Prentice-Hall, 1965), 105.
2. Alexander Jackson Davis, "Advertisement," *Rural Residences: Consisting of designs, original and selected, for cottages, farm-houses, villas, and village churches: with brief explanations, estimates, and a specification of materials, construction, etc.* (1837; facs. New York: Da Capo Press, 1980), n.p.
3. Andrew Jackson Downing, *A Treatise on the Theory and Practice of Landscape Gardening Adapted to North America* (1841; New York: C. M. Saxton & Co., 1855), 376.
4. Wright designed site-specific Usonian houses for middle-class clients. Frank Lloyd Wright, *The Natural House* (New York: Horizon Press, 1954), 91.
5. Vincent J. Scully, *The Shingle Style: Architectural Theory and Design from Richardson to the Origins of Wright* (New Haven: Yale University Press, 1955), 163–64.
6. Steven Holl, *Anchoring* (New York: Princeton Architectural Press, 1989), 9.
7. Cole, "Essay on American Scenery," 100.

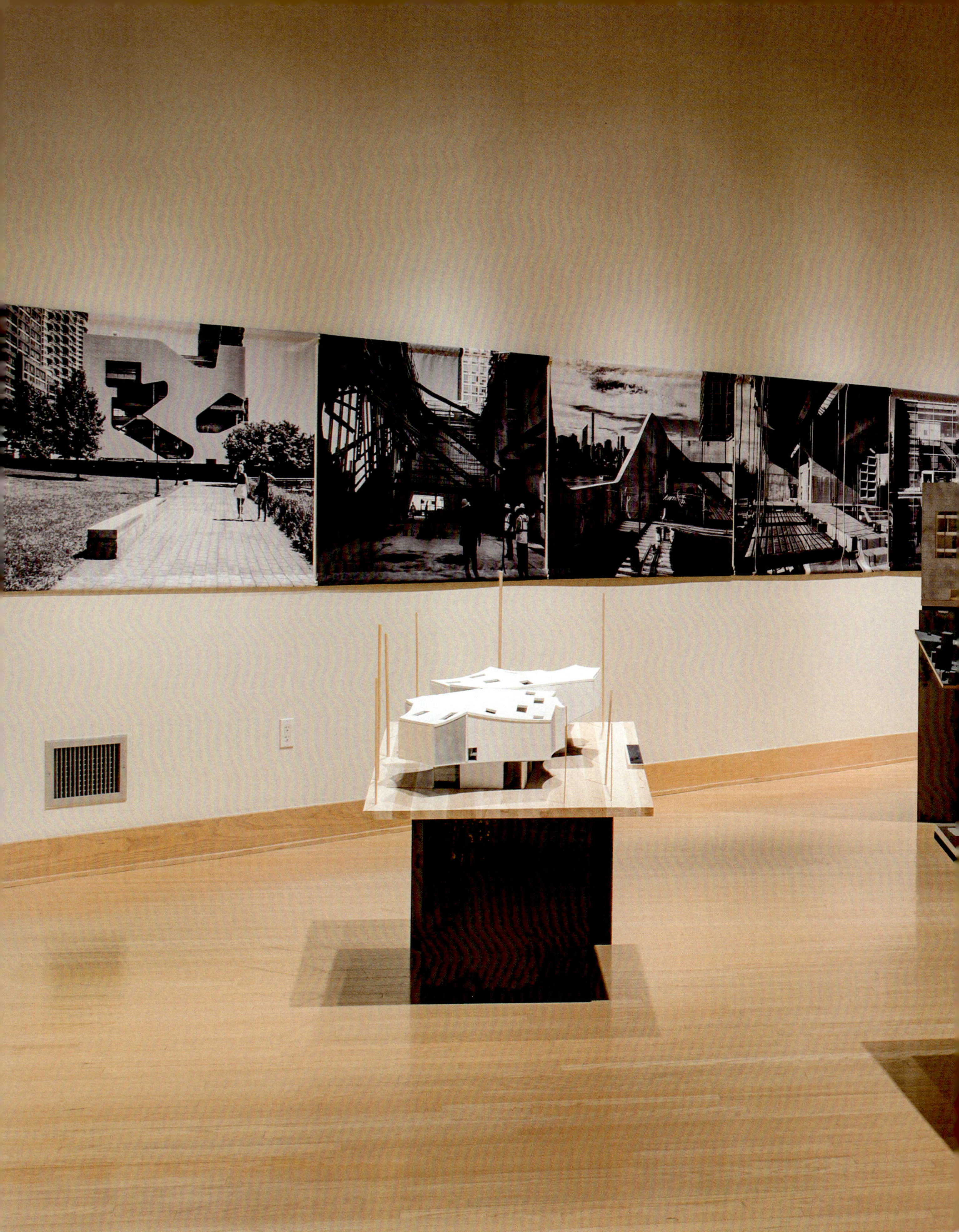

Installation view, *Steven Holl: Making Architecture*,
Samuel Dorsky Museum of Art, New Paltz, New York,
February 10–July 15, 2018.

Photo courtesy of The Dorsky Museum. Photograph by Bob Wagner.

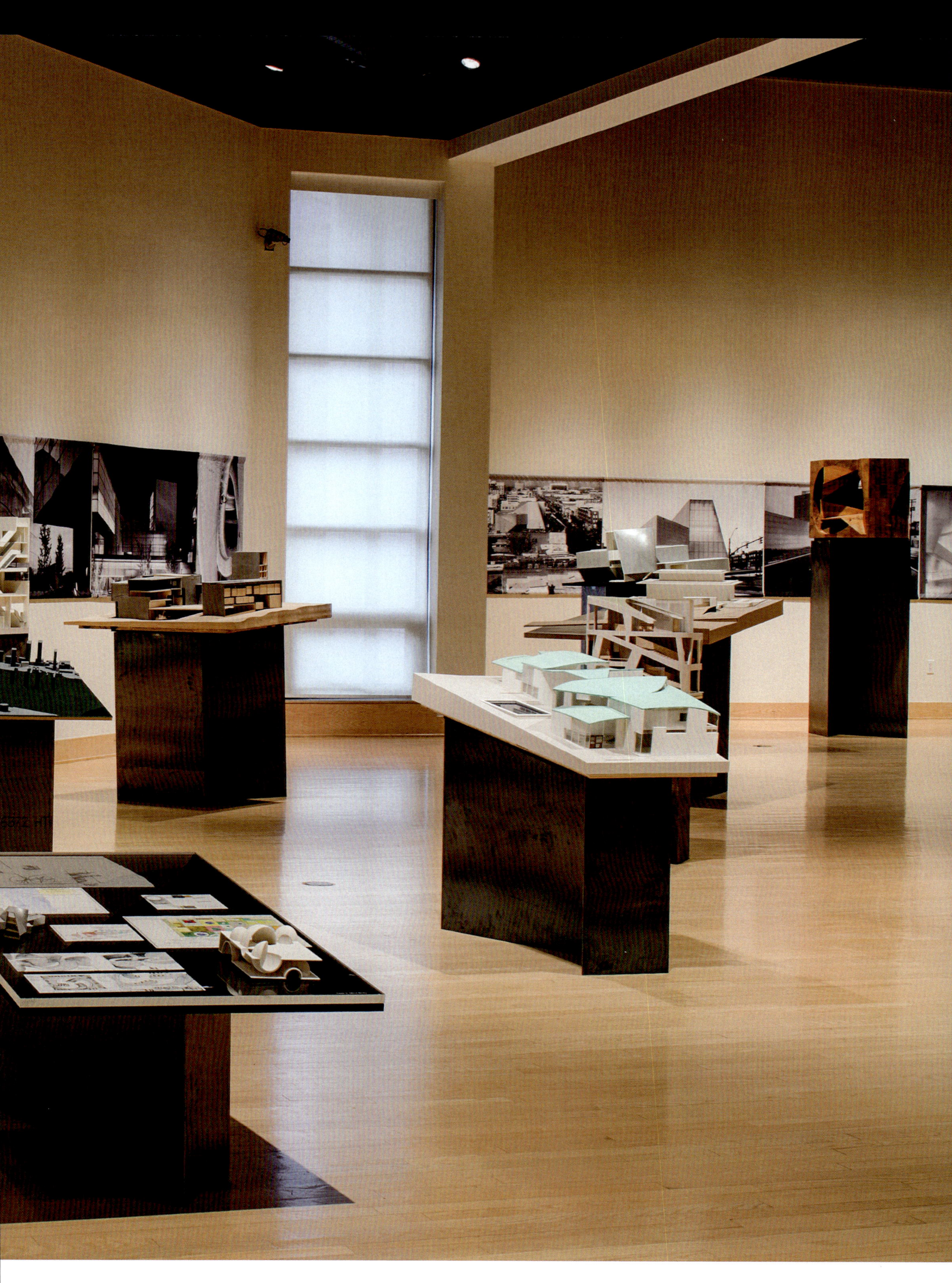

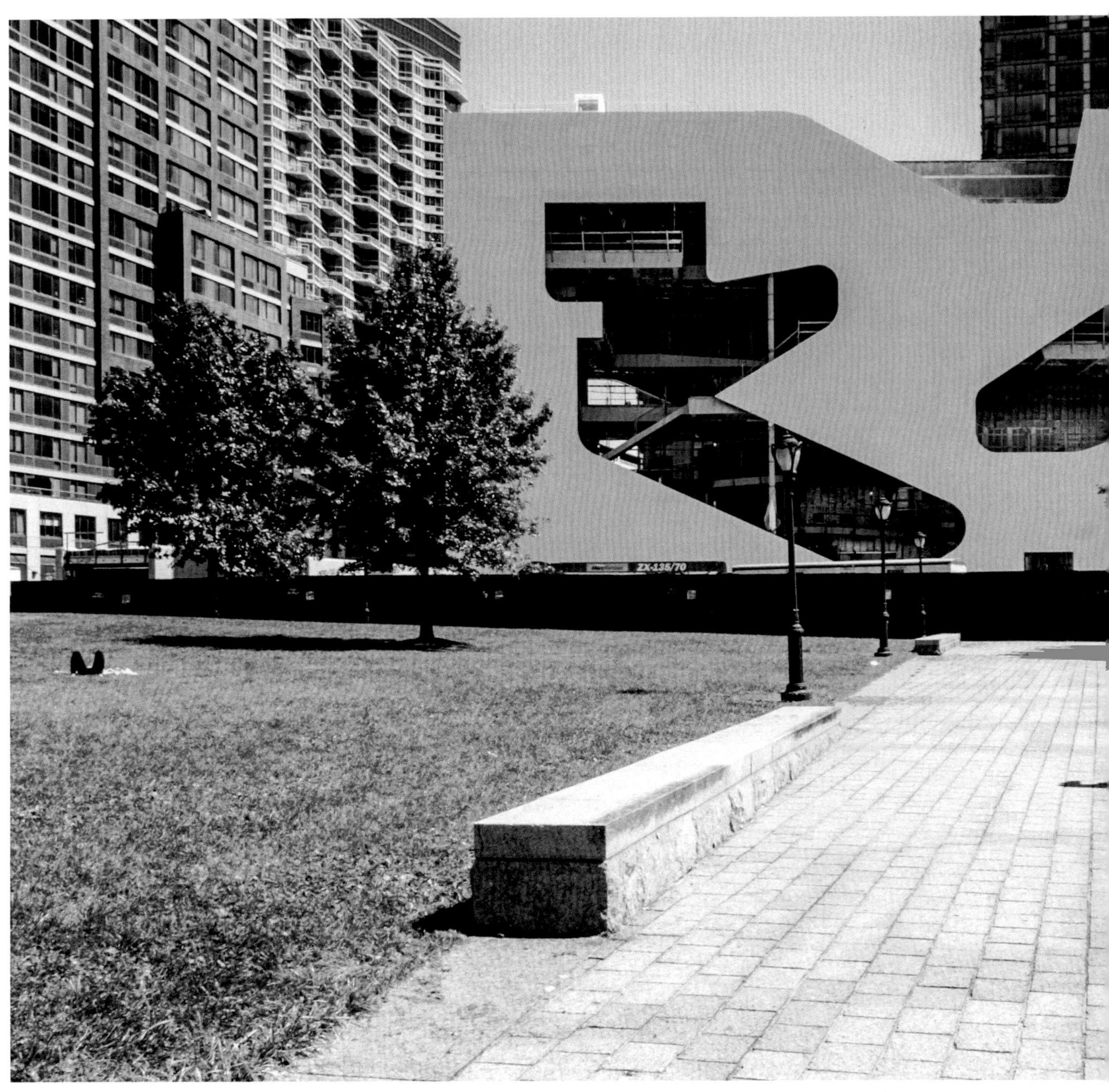

Steven Holl Architects, Hunters Point Library, 2017.
Photograph © Paul Warchol,
courtesy of Steven Holl Architects.

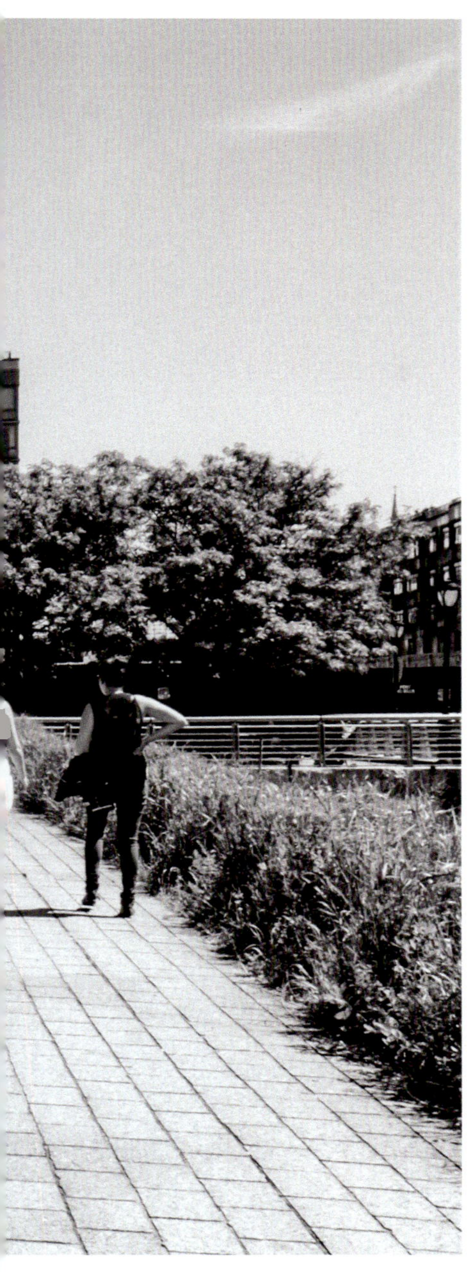

RECONFIGURING ARCHITECTURAL AGENCY

Peter Olshavsky

Set on twenty-eight acres of stunning rural landscape in Rhinebeck, New York, Steven Holl's Ex of IN House (2016) began as an exploration of the notion of "In." Through iterative geometric exercises that studied spherical intersections coupled with a partial tesseract, Holl resolved the resulting spatial conditions, programmatically and materially, as a small guesthouse (fig. 49). To accompany the physical process of this exploration, the architect developed a seven-point manifesto. In this text, Holl proposes that architecture should be "freed from the purely objective," so that it can have an "elemental force of sensual beauty."[1] As demonstrated in the sumptuous wood and glass interior of this exploratory house, the architect notes, the power of this approach does not arise from its function. Nor should it be viewed as architecture reduced to a mere object. Its elemental force or agency is more complex.

This example from Holl's recent work hints at a deeper truth about the architect's position: when done well, architecture has the profound ability to alter "the way you can see, the way you can feel,"[2] and more. Placing us at the intersection

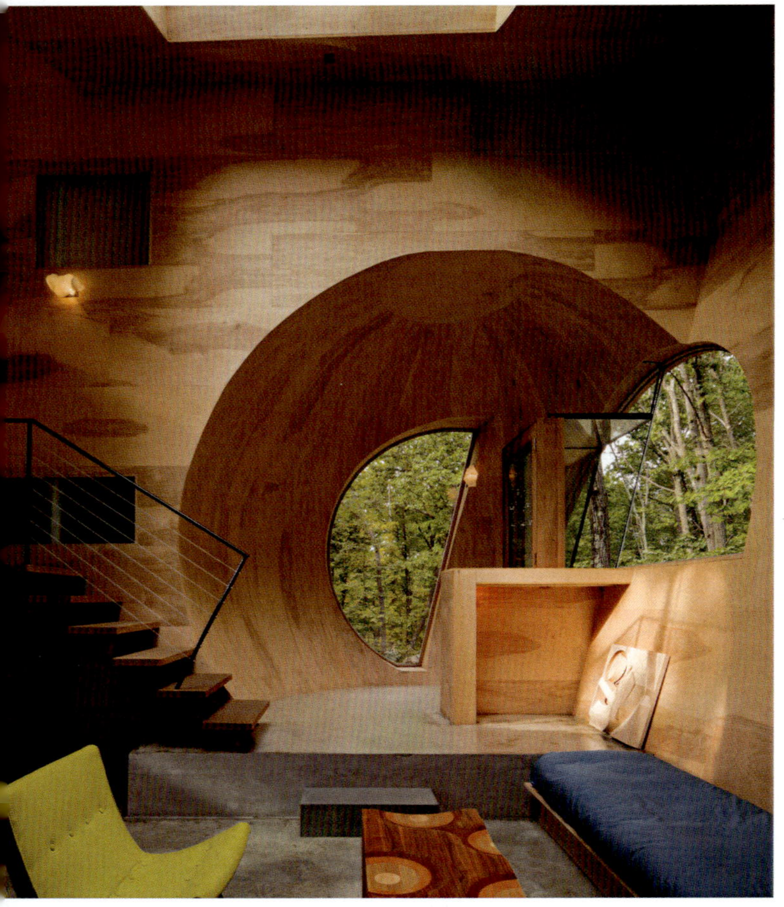

of the relationship between bodies and buildings, architectural agency is crucial to phenomenology and to Holl's purposeful engagement with this tradition.

CONTEXT

Architectural phenomenology appears in the middle of the twentieth century as a broad set of priorities that first found resonance with individuals—Christian Norberg-Schulz, Charles Moore, and Kenneth Frampton—working in architecture history and practice. Modulating the modernist belief that techno-sciences are primary driving forces for architecture, the first generation espoused phenomenology by opening themselves to existential questioning and embodied agency in an effort to reground architectural discourse.[3] Consequentially, they initiated a varied and lasting architectural tradition that drew on philosophy to make their case.

Developing decades earlier than its architectural counterpart, philosophical phenomenology emerged in its modern sense from Edmond Husserl's Logical Investigations (1900–1901).[4] Husserl arrived at new insights about structures of consciousness in the world and set in place descriptive practices that would influence later philosophers, including Martin Heidegger, Maurice Merleau-Ponty, Hannah Arendt, and Paul Ricœur, among others. This philosophical work, as a variety of what is now dubbed "continental" philosophy, would find fertile soil with the post-WWII generation in Europe and North America. Alongside this geographic expansion, the scope and practices of phenomenology have also diversified to address both perennial and topical concerns.[5] Philosophers and academics continue to cultivate work in a global context that is reliant on or extends questions, insights, and practices from phenomenology.

From the inception of this approach, advocates of phenomenology produced work that was far from monolithic. Yet, we can recognize common concerns. They seek to address issues as they relate to human experience. To broach a particular issue, they

fig. 49

Steven Holl Architects, Ex of IN House, Rhinebeck, New York, 2016. Photograph by Paul Warchol, courtesy of Steven Holl Architects.

set their argumentation in its textual and historical context rather than addressing the subject as a discreet problem. By examining an issue in this way, philosophical discourse becomes a means to produce a "crisis."[6] In Husserl's work crisis appears in the rift between science's "mathematization of nature" and everyday life practices. Crisis for Merleau-Ponty emerges in the problematic separation of mind and body and body and world. Identifying and unpacking a crisis makes possible a philosopher's work of relearning how to look at the world from a perspective not complicit in the crisis. Through processes of inquiry and redescription, they attain the understanding necessary to reimagine aspects of the world.

When it comes to imagining things differently, of course, architects took notice of the possibilities. Steven Holl was among them. His embrace of phenomenology occurred rather abruptly. Immersed in education and practice during the predominance of postmodernism in the United States and Europe, Holl became disillusioned with the typological research he was pursuing in the vein of the Italian Rationalist Alberto Sartoris that was characteristic of the period.[7] Then, in the winter of 1984, he had a fortuitous encounter with a philosopher traveling across Canada, who introduced him to phenomenology and the work of Merleau-Ponty.[8] Holl would go on to engage phenomenology in architecture as a philosophical orientation. This position began as no mere transcription of philosophy into architecture. With interlocutors like Kenneth Frampton, Juhani Pallasmaa, and Alberto Pérez-Gómez, Holl sought to work out an alternative understanding of the discipline and its future through histories, theories, and innovative architectural projects. These phenomenological pursuits have resulted in a successful design practice that has built elegant and acclaimed works around the globe.

The depth and purpose of Holl's engagement with this orientation is sometimes overshadowed by his careful attention to qualitative lighting, tactile surfaces, bespoke details, human proportions, and graceful atmospheres that come to the forefront of experiences with his projects (fig. 50). Focusing only on the phenomenal, as if architectural phenomenology can be reduced to this, he argues, has its limits. "Though many if not most people who appreciate my work," Holl says, "seem to focus on its experiential

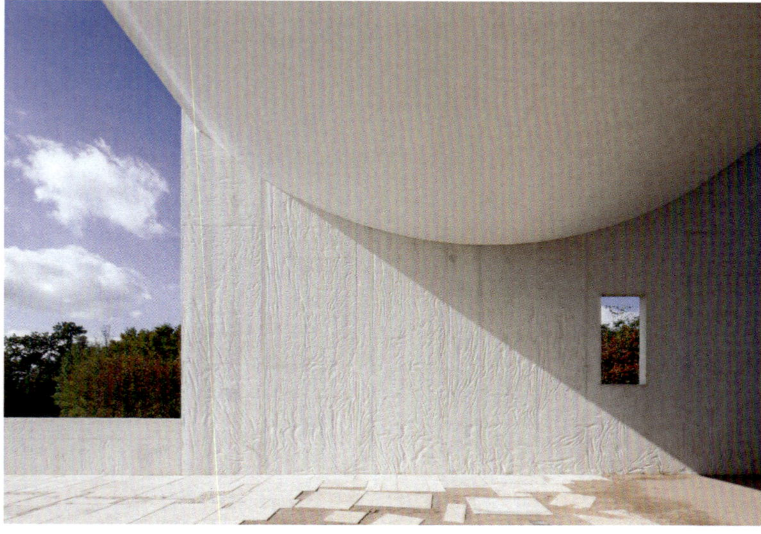

fig. 50

Steven Holl Architects, Herning Museum of Contemporary Art, Herning, Denmark, 2009. Photograph courtesy of Iwan Baan.

or phenomenological qualities—the light, the use of materials, and so forth,"[9] this fixation reduces the work to the mere objects of architecture. "[W]hat is important," he goes on to say, "is the idea."[10] Ideas underpin and guide architectural making. We see this ideation through his watercolors, sketches, models, and other modes of production by his project teams seeking the "phenomenal potential of ideas."[11]

Whether pursuing "luminist space" or the possibilities of "liquid light," ideas are part and parcel of larger phenomenological questions.[12] It is through these broader inquiries that Holl's identification of crisis in the phenomenological tradition becomes visible. He is troubled by the proliferation of construction that is artificial, passive, and mute, or "banality in excess." He sees danger in architecture that shows "indifference to quality of life."[13] To put it simply, crisis for Holl emerges in the reduction of architecture to a mere object. Holl's work from a phenomenological orientation can thus be described as a purposeful engagement to redress this crisis.

RECONFIGURATION

Reading across Holl's four decades of production, we see him working to learn to look at the world differently. His effort is rooted in the primacy of human experience. Through the body, as Merleau-Ponty maintains, "the perceived world is the always presupposed foundation of all rationality, all value and all existence."[14] As a locus of intentional action, it has been foundational in nearly everything Holl has done from the mid-1980s onward, including explorations of "parallax," "haptic architecture," and "porosity." What it means to be embodied is a deep and abiding point of departure for his thinking, making, and reflecting on architecture.[15]

Intimately linked to embodied experience, agency is mobilized in a non-traditional way as a powerful insight for his approach. To be an embodied human is to possess agency, or the capacity to think, feel, and act. This sense of humanness has historically been defined by its categorical difference to non-humans' lack of agency.[16] In recent decades, however, some philosophers have questioned this older anthropocentric conception and reconfigured agency's scope. Matter, things, and technologies are increasingly seen as co-constitutive of human agency.[17] This includes architecture.

By the time Holl published the essay "Edge of a City" in 1991, we find a similar reconfiguration of agency in his work. He imagines an "architecture [that] changes the way we live," one that "alters our experience of time of day or season" and changes our "mood and bodily temperature."[18] Like a tuning fork compelled into synchronous vibration by another tuning fork struck nearby, bodies resonate with architecture. Architecture in this sense actively shapes the body's access to the world in sensuous ways. The human capacity for thinking, feeling, and acting in the world is co-constituted by architecture. In the work, Holl carefully elaborates this hybrid form of agency, in both its metaphoric and material aspects, as a corrective to the crisis in architecture that he identified.

Starting with metaphor, we find numerous examples in Holl's work. "Intertwining" and "enmeshing" are driving notions for the Rubenstein Commons (begun 2015), a work in progress at the famed Institute for Advanced

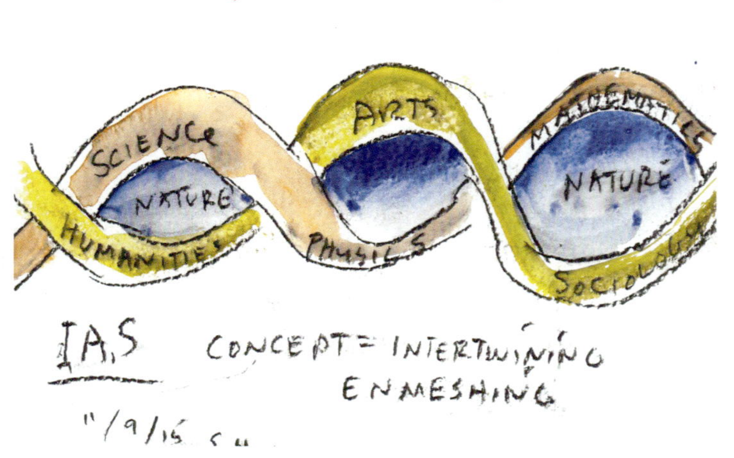

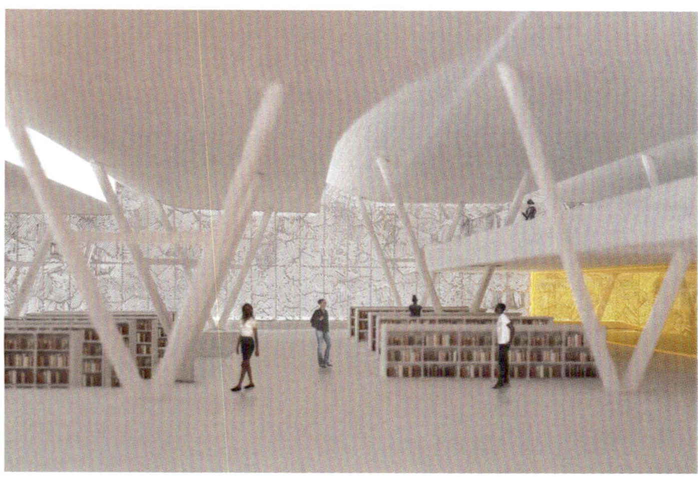

Study in Princeton, New Jersey (fig. 51). These suggest important entanglements between nature, architecture, and the community of scholars in reflection. The Arts Building West (2006) on the campus of the University of Iowa, Holl says, is "half human, half scientific," while the university's more recent, nearby Visual Arts Building (2016), is "an agent for change," according to Chris McVoy, senior partner at Steven Holl Architects.[19]

The language used in these examples is more than anthropomorphism or a series of rhetorical flourishes. It is crucial to articulate particular ways bodies and buildings relate. This is because metaphor in Holl's work underpins the reconfiguration of agency. "[S]eeing as," Paul Ricœur says, founds and organizes life in an "imagistic fullness" that leads to a manner of being.[20] Metaphor redescribes what it refers to so that imagined possibilities can be acted upon. Such descriptions are, as George Lakoff and Mark Johnson call them, "metaphors we live by."[21] As systematic figurative concepts, these metaphors lead the older view of agency awry. They found a conception in which human agency and architecture cannot be easily disentangled.

In further examining Holl's elaboration of agency, architectural matter also has a vital efficacy. In the Malawi Library (designed 2017) on a new campus in Lilongwe, architectural agency can be appreciated in the way the work manifests specific microclimates for daily life. The roof extends beyond the library's enclosure to form an arcade on all sides, breaking the high-sun angle to block solar heat and deflect heavy precipitation during rainy season. This affords qualitative space that urges us to move along or linger at the building's edges. On the interior (fig. 52), the curved roof blades and bamboo-screened

fig. 51

Steven Holl, *Intertwining Enmeshing*, Rubenstein Commons, Institute for Advanced Studies, Princeton, New Jersey, 2015, watercolor on paper. Courtesy of Steven Holl Architects.

fig. 52

Steven Holl Architects, Malawi Library, Liongwe, Malawi, 2017. Photomontage courtesy of Steven Holl Architects.

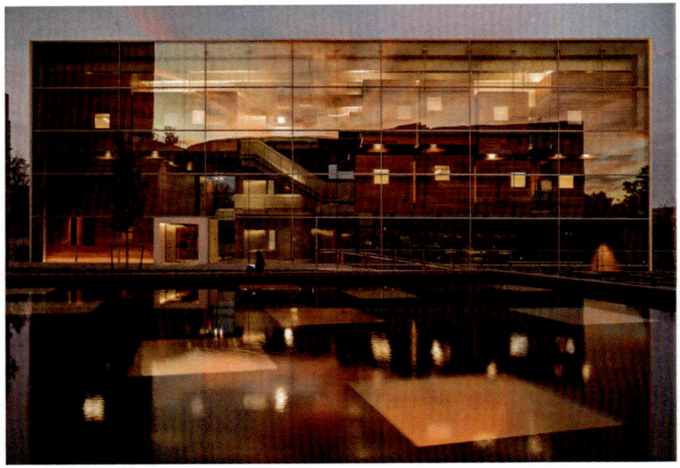

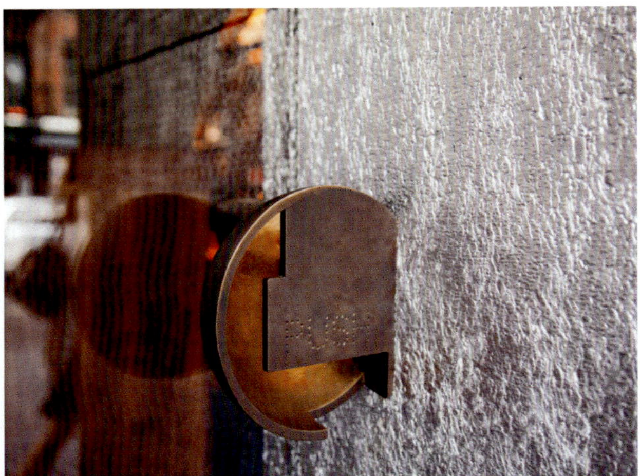

façades limit solar heat gain, but are fashioned to use cross ventilation to temper the southeast African climate, enabling thermal comfort for our actions. All of these elements support the work of the library staff and visitors to expand the access and production of knowledge in the developing nation.

At the Lewis Center for the Arts (2017) on the southern edge of the campus of Princeton University, the architectural form of the new arts complex, programmatic organization, and atmospheres impress their subtle influences on the body. On the exterior of the music building, the cherry-wood practice rooms are visibly nested within a glass enclosure and suspended on steel rods to create acoustic separation (fig. 53). Their forms and fenestration draw our thoughts to their notational arrangement and the private routines of practice held within them.

Music also arises from the elemental force of the Reid Building (2014) for the Glasgow School of Art. At the center of the project, cylindrical voids organize the volume, enabling light, ventilation, and circulation into the depth of the floor plate to actively support the work of the faculty and students. The agency of these architectural elements has beckoned the school's music students to hold impromptu concerts in the multi-story resonating chambers, saturating academic life in music.

This intention is also carried through in details and elements. Holl's artfully crafted door handles are a highly illustrative example of a detail with sensuous force. The cast silicone bronze half-spherical handles (fig. 54) at the Editions de Parfum Frédéric Malle (2014) in New York greet the hands of visitors to the shop, momentarily drawing our thought to this pre-reflective task that enables us to move from outside to inside. Holl's attention to the elements of primary stairs and

fig. 53

Steven Holl Architects, Lewis Arts Complex, Princeton University, Princeton, New Jersey, 2017. Photograph courtesy of Paul Warchol.

fig. 54

Steven Holl Architects, door handle of Editions de Parfums Frédéric Malle, New York, New York, 2014. Photograph courtesy of Susan Wides.

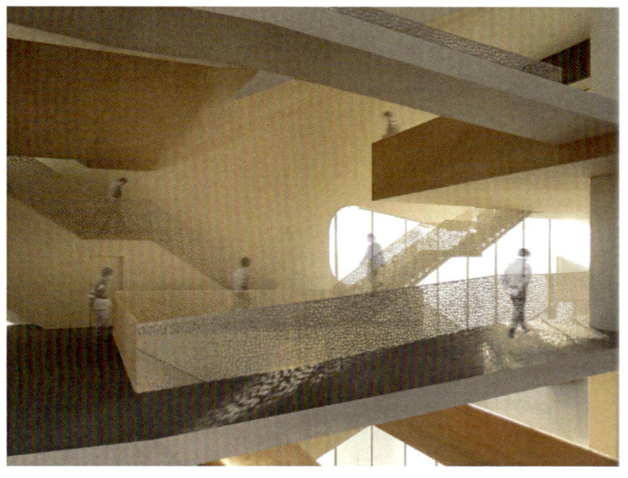

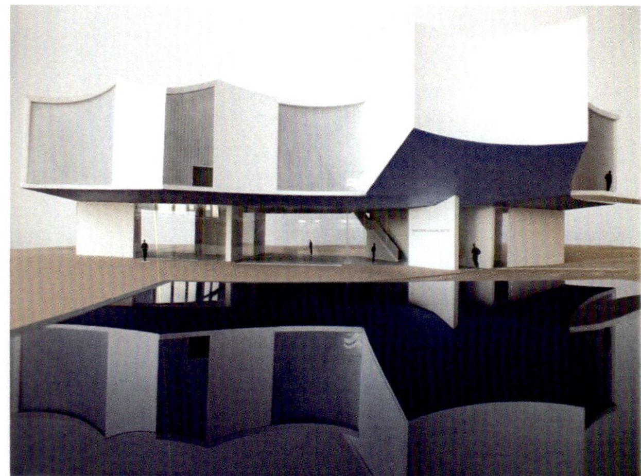

ramps also manifests architecture's agency. In works like Hunters Point Community Library (2017) in Queens, or Maggie's Cancer Care Centre at St. Barts (2017) in London, these elements are spatially generous and gracefully proportioned for our bodies in motion (fig. 55). They are compositionally dynamic and animate the play of diurnal light on and through their forms and patterned material assemblies. The comfortable scale of these elements encourages our social interactions. For the able-bodied, they propel us to ascend and descend rather than seek out the elevator.

A second, more direct example from Princeton's Lewis Center, is no less descriptive of this agenda, is a tilted mirrored surface that was proposed for the theater building's back of house.[22] This design element was meant to alter the dancers' self-perception, making them appear taller and leaner just before they went on stage. This shows architecture actively altering the dancers' conscious state. The philosopher Alva Noë explains, "Consciousness isn't something that happens inside us: it is something that we do, actively, in our dynamic interaction with the world around us."[23] Consciousness is deeply interwoven with the built environment, which challenges (or supports) the autonomy of humans.

This is also elaborated at the Fine Arts Building (begun 2016) at Franklin and Marshall College in Lancaster, Pennsylvania. The building's massing is lifted to place the studios among the mature tree canopy on campus. To the east of the project, the reflecting pool, which can also handle storm water overflow, offers an inversion of the lofted architecture in the pool's watery hues. This mirror image (fig. 56) is meant to take hold of its campus audience and create a "special articulation" of place.[24] While mirror images teach us about the body's perception, Merleau-

fig. 55

Steven Holl Architects, Hunters Point Community Library, Queens, New York, 2017. Photomontage courtesy of Steven Holl Architects.

fig. 56

Steven Holl Architects, *Model*, Winter Visual Arts Center, Franklin & Marshall College, Lancaster, Pennsylvania, 2016, resin-impregnated plaster 3D print and acrylic on chipboard base. Courtesy of Steven Holl Architects.

Ponty notes, they also show us "what things saw" of us.[25] Here, we are directly reminded of architecture's role in our lives in the uncanny way it looks back.

What all of these instances tell us, in their various ways, is that Holl's architectural works alter the reductive view that humans are sovereign actors set apart from the world. Rather, Holl puts forward a hybrid agency intertwining flesh, glass, steel, and wood. While the architect intends and achieves certain affects, these can never be entirely foreseen or circumscribed. Architecture's agency always exceeds intentions when placed in public. That is to say, architecture's agency only appears when coupled with bodies in space and time. As a socially embedded artifact, this coupling opens sensuous possibilities that reach both inward to change our internal make up and extend our humanness beyond our skin.

VIA THE WORK

Drawing attention to the ways Holl's work figures an expanded notion of agency shows what might otherwise remain hidden, namely the capacity of architecture to prompt people to think, feel, and act in ways particular to it. This conception does not assign agency to architecture as if it were identical to humans, but makes intelligible the entangled relationships between embodied subjects and architecture as an effect of ongoing social–material practices of making architecture.

Situating Holl's work within his broader engagement with phenomenology, we come to realize that his earlier notion—"architecture changes the way we live"—no longer goes far enough. Addressing the crisis of architecture, the deliberate metaphoric and material aspects of agency expose a more profound role for the discipline. "My own words take me by surprise," Merleau-Ponty wisely says, "and teach me what to think."[26] In the ongoing relationship between bodies and buildings, Holl's architecture now more than ever takes us by surprise and teaches us to see the world through the work. Perhaps this explains why, as he observes, a number of his projects start contentiously.[27] With time the best of his architecture, like the Nelson-Atkins Museum (2007) in Kansas City, goes on to found and organize people's lives in ways that make it impossible to conceive of the world without the work. This reconfiguration leaves us with a bold insight: architecture makes us what we are.

NOTES

1. Steven Holl Architects, "Ex of IN House: A Conversation with Steven Holl and Dimitra Tsachrelia," video, 0:55 min., posted January 13, 2017, http://www.stevenholl.com/videos.
2. Steven Holl Architects, "Ex of IN House."
3. Jorge Otero-Pailos, *Architecture's Historical Turn: Phenomenology and the Rise of the Postmodern* (Minneapolis: University of Minnesota Press, 2010).
4. Simon Critchley, *Continental Philosophy: A Very Short Introduction* (Oxford: Oxford University Press, 2001), 13.
5. Dan Zahavi, ed., *The Oxford Handbook of Contemporary Phenomenology* (Oxford: Oxford University Press, 2013).
6. Critchley, *Continental Philosophy*, 72–74.
7. Steven Holl, *Pamphlet Architecture 9: Rural and Urban House Types in North America* (New York: Princeton Architectural Press, 1982).
8. Yehuda E. Safran, "Steven Holl: Idea and Method," in *Steven Holl: Idea and Phenomena*, Steven Holl et al. (Baden: Lars Müller, 2002), 78.
9. Richard C. Levine and Fernando Marques Cecilia, eds., *El Croquis 93: Steven Holl: 1996–1999* (Madrid: El Croquis Editorial, 1999), 73.
10. Levine and Cecilia, *El Croquis 93*, 73.
11. Richard C. Levine and Fernando Marques Cecilia, eds., *El Croquis 78: Steven Holl: 1986–1996* (Madrid: El Croquis Editorial, 1996), 18.
12. Andrew Caruso, "Steven Holl: Not a 'Signature' Architecture (And Why That is Good)," *National Building Museum*, May 29, 2012, https://www.nbm.org/steven-holl-not-signature-architect-thats-good.
13. Steven Holl, *Parallax* (New York: Princeton Architectural Press, 2000), 175.
14. Maurice Merleau-Ponty, *The Primacy of Perception and Other Essays on Phenomenological Psychology, the Philosophy of Art, History, and Politics* (Evanston, IL: Northwestern University Press, 1964), 13.
15. Holl, *Parallax*, 26.
16. Anthony Giddens and Christopher Pierson, *A Conversation with Anthony Giddens: Making Sense of Modernity* (Stanford, CA: Stanford University Press, 1998), 88.
17. Peter Kroes and Peter-Paul Verbeek, eds., The Moral Status of Technical Artefacts (Dordrecht: Springer, 2014), 5.
18. Steven Holl, "Edge of a City," in *Pamphlet Architecture 13: Edge of a City* (New York: Princeton Architectural Press, 1991), 12.
19. Steven Holl Architects, "Visual Arts Building, University of Iowa: A Conversation with Steven Holl and Chris McVoy," video, 7:00 min., posted March 14, 2017, http://www.stevenholl.com/videos.
20. Paul Ricœur, *The Rule of Metaphor: Multi-disciplinary Studies of the Creation of Meaning in Language* (London: Routledge, 2003), 252.
21. George Lakoff and Mark Johnson, *Metaphors We Live By* (Chicago: University of Chicago Press, 2003), 55.
22. Janell Rock (BNIM, interior designer on Lewis Center for the Arts), in discussion with the author, Kansas City, MO, November 3, 2017.
23. Alva Noë, *Out of Our Heads: Why You Are Not Your Brain, and Other Lessons from the Biology of Consciousness* (New York: Wang and Hill, 2009), 24.
24. Steven Holl Architects, "Fine Arts Building—Franklin and Marshall," accessed November 28, 2017, http://www.stevenholl.com/projects/franklin-&-marshall.
25. Merleau-Ponty, *The Primacy of Perception*, 168–69.
26. Maurice Merleau-Ponty, *Signs*, trans. Richard C. McCleary (Evanston, IL: Northwestern University Press, 1964), 88.
27. Steven Holl, "Steven Holl Architects," lecture, the Mary Atkins Lecture Series, Kansas City, MO, November 2, 2017.

STEVEN HOLL: MAKING ARCHITECTURE

PROJECTS

LEWIS CENTER FOR THE ARTS

Princeton University, New Jersey
2007–2017

The program design for the Lewis Center for the Arts includes a theater and dance building, an arts building, and a music building with rehearsal and practice rooms. The three buildings are joined together in a new quadrangle by a gathering forum sited below ground, under the central reflecting pool. The project creates a new campus gateway, shaping interactive spaces while maximizing porosity (openness to the possibility of many functions) and movement from all sides.

Overlooking views into the dance and theater practice spaces and the orchestral rehearsal space are designed to provoke curiosity and enhance interaction among the students and faculty. As an open invitation to the public, the new quadrangle connects the local community to the university. Holl developed each of the three buildings' interiors uniquely. The Wallace Theater and Dance Building is based on the idea of a "thing within a thing" (a rectangle in a circle). Within the overall concrete frame, the black-box theater is made of steel, while the dance theaters are made of foamed aluminum, whitewashed wood, and board-formed concrete. A "dancing stair," with a guardrail made of CNC-milled, perforated steel that follows a pattern inspired by Laban dance notation, connects all the floors.

Holl refers to the structuring thought of the Arts Building as an "embedded concept" with its concrete and stone tower connecting to Princeton's historic Blair Arch.

The principal idea behind the Music Building is "suspension." Here, above the large orchestral rehearsal room, individual practice rooms are suspended on steel rods. Acoustically separate, these individual wooden chambers have a resonant quality.

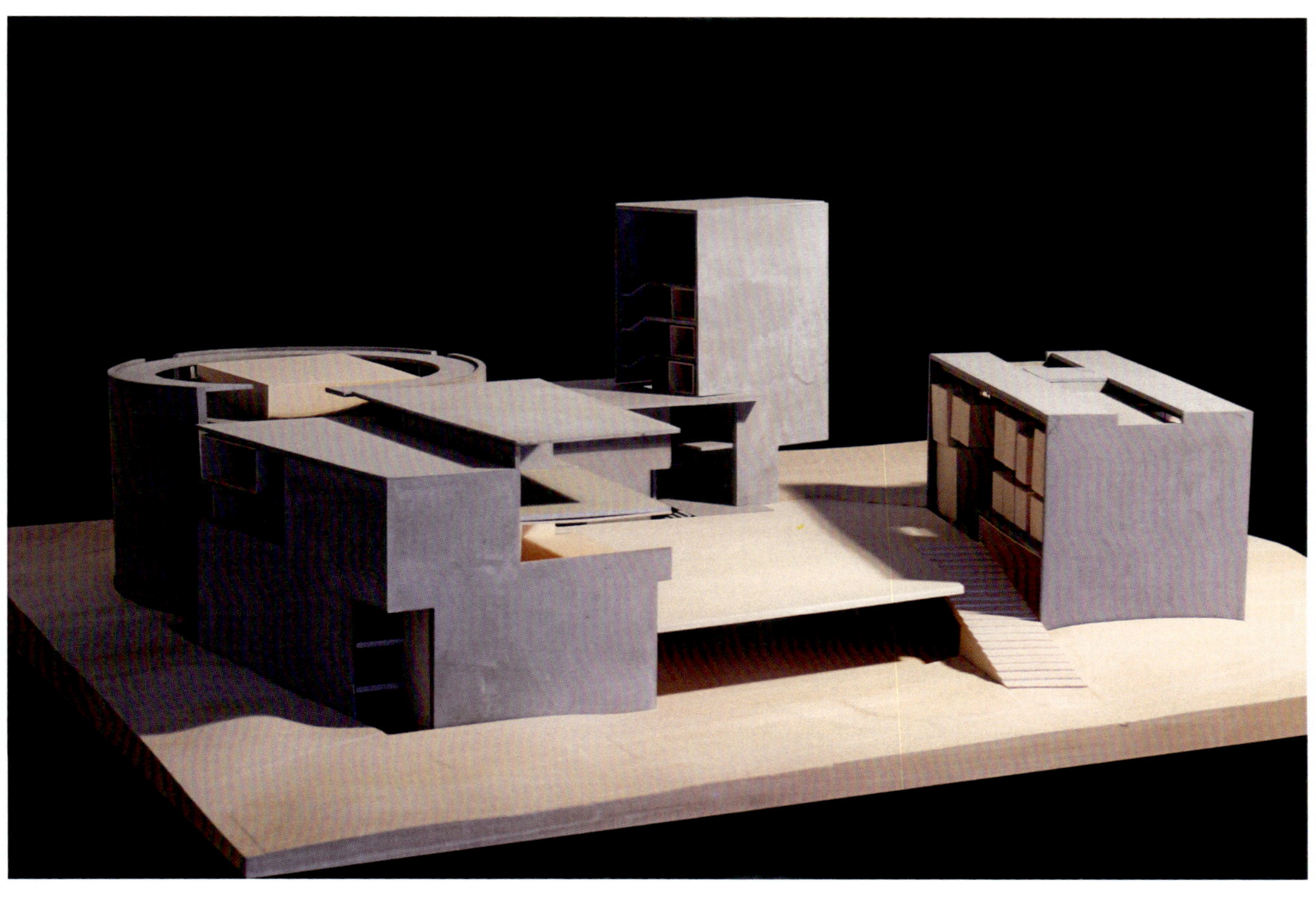

Steven Holl Architects, *Lewis Center for the Arts Model at Night, Princeton University, 2007*, model. Courtesy of Steven Holl Architects.

HUNTERS POINT COMMUNITY LIBRARY

Queens, New York
2010–2018

Located on a prominent site along the East River, against the backdrop of recently built skyscraper condominiums, the new 22,000-square-foot Queens Library at Hunters Point serves as both a public building and public park, and will bring community-devoted space to the increasingly privatized Long Island City waterfront.

The concrete structure of the building is exposed and aluminum painted, giving the exterior a subtle sparkle. A golden-section upturned rectangle carved out of the façade reflects the browsing circuit of movement within the interior of the library, with glazed cuts granting users unique views of the city as they move up a series of bookshelf-flanked stairs. The main Manhattan view, perpendicular to the internal movement of the library, provides visitors to this small space with a dramatic experience.

The program's separation into a children's area, teen area, and adult area can be read in the sculpted cuts of the east face of the building, one façade opening for each area. Despite the separations, the programmatic divisions are fluid. While the plan is compact, the building section of the new library is open and flowing, allowing for the most energy-efficient design and the greatest amount of public green space on the site.

On the east entrance side, the library faces a reading garden bordered by a low park office pavilion with a grove of ginkgo trees. Ascending the staircase inside, visitors can reach a rooftop reading garden with panoramic views of the city. At night, the glowing presence of the new library along the waterfront joins the Pepsi sign and the "Long Island" sign at the Gantry Plaza State Park as a beacon for this resurgent community.

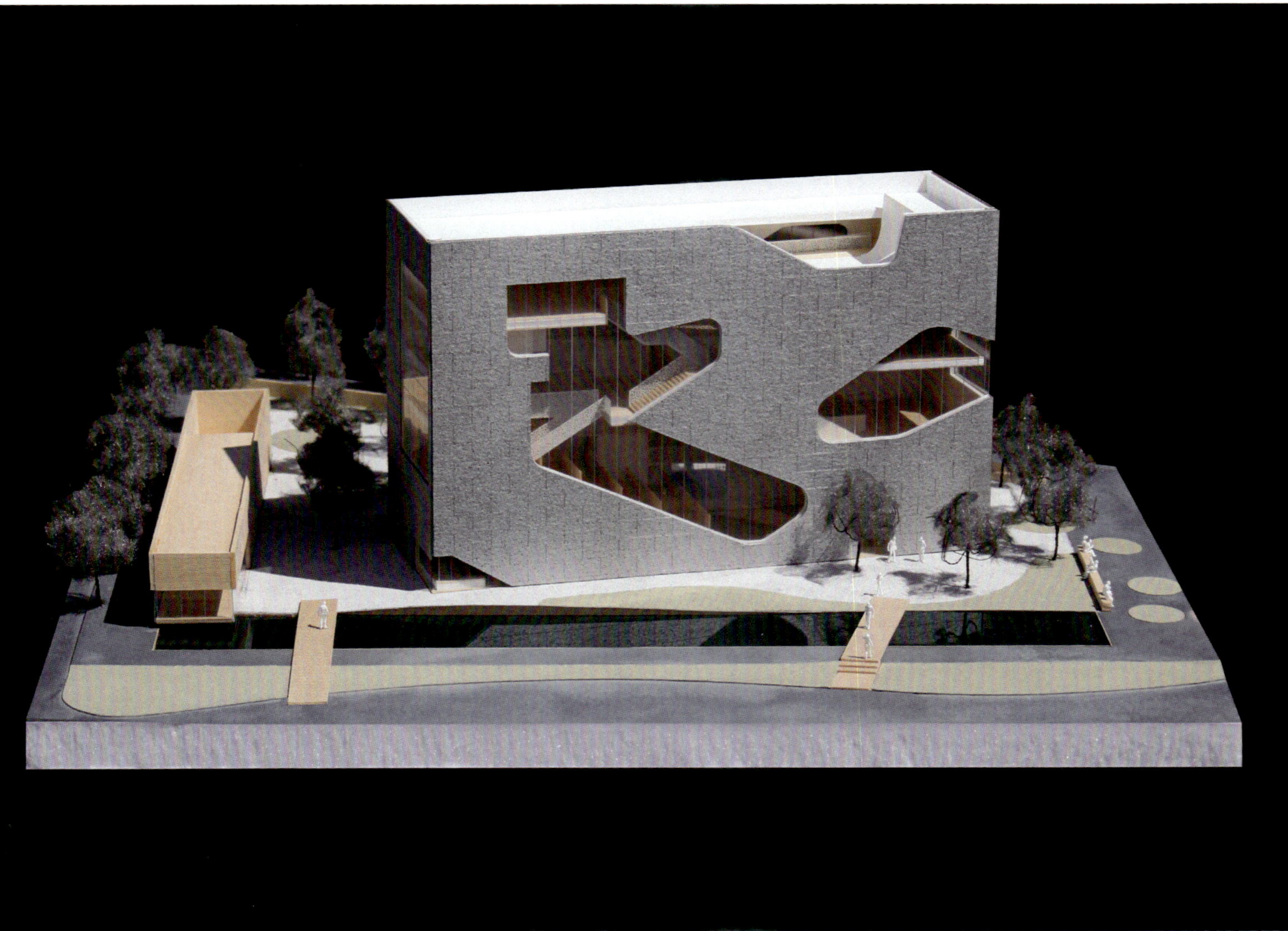

Steven Holl Architects, *Hunters Point Library*, 2017, model. Photograph courtesy of Paul Warchol.

MAGGIE'S CANCER CARE CENTRE

London, England
2011–2017

Maggie's Cancer Care Centre is located on a historic site in the center of London, adjacent to the large courtyard of St. Bartholomew's Hospital. The oldest hospital in London, it was established in 1123, at the same time as St. Bartholomew the Great church. Both the church and the hospital were founded by the priest Rahere "for the restoration of poor men." Layers of history characterize this unique site, connecting it deeply to the medieval culture of London.

While most of the realized healthcare facilities at Maggie's Centre have been horizontal buildings, the building at St. Barts is vertical. It replaces a pragmatic 1960s brick structure adjacent to a seventeenth-century stone structure by James Gibbs, which contains the "Great Hall" and the famous Hogarth staircase.

Holl's building is envisioned as a "vessel within a vessel within a vessel." The structure is a branching concrete frame; the inner layer is perforated bamboo, and the outer layer is matte white glass with colored glass fragments that recall the neume notation of medieval music of the thirteenth century. The word neume, originating from the Greek *pneuma*, means "vital force"—it suggests a "breath of life" that fills one with inspiration like a stream of air or the blowing of the wind. The outer glass layer is organized in horizontal bands, like a musical staff, while the concrete structure branches out like a hand. The three-story building has an open, curved staircase integral to the concrete frame, with open spaces vertically lined in perforated bamboo. The glass façade, made of horizontal strips, follows the geometry of the main stair along the north façade, then lifts up with clear glass to face the main square, marking the main front entry. There is a second entry on the west, opening to the extended garden of the adjacent church.

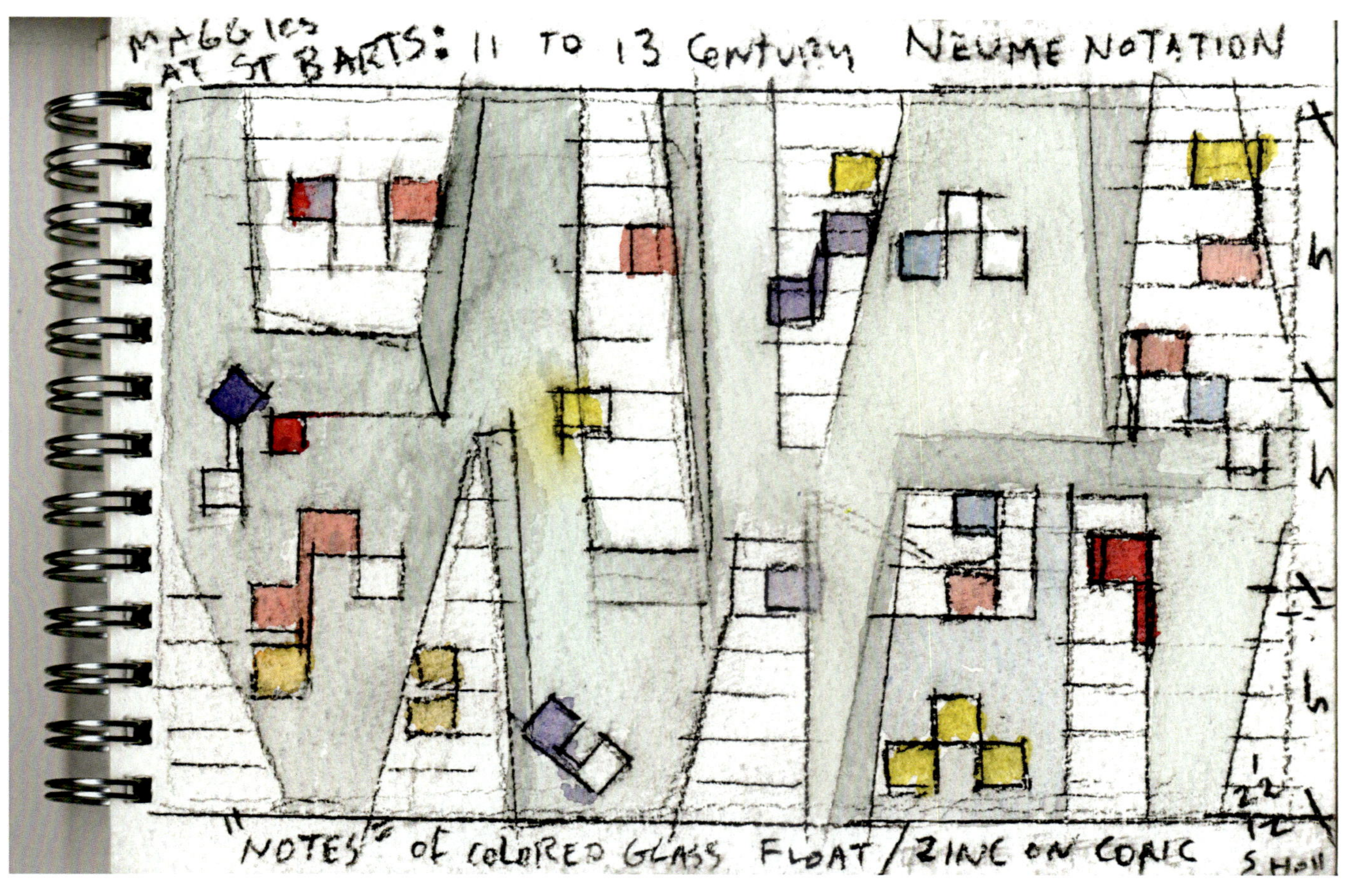

Steven Holl, *Notes of Colored Glass 01/21/2012*, 2012, watercolor on paper. Courtesy of Steven Holl.

INSTITUTE FOR CONTEMPORARY ART
VIRGINIA COMMONWEALTH UNIVERSITY
Richmond, Virginia
2011–2017

Situated at the edge of the Virginia Commonwealth University campus, on Richmond's busiest intersection, the new Institute for Contemporary Art is designed to link the university with the surrounding community, forming a gateway to the university with an inviting sense of openness.

The main entrance is created by an intersection of the performance space and forum, adding a "Z" component to the "X–Y" movement of the intersection. The torsion of these intersecting bodies is joined by what Holl calls a "plane of the present" to galleries that exist in "forking

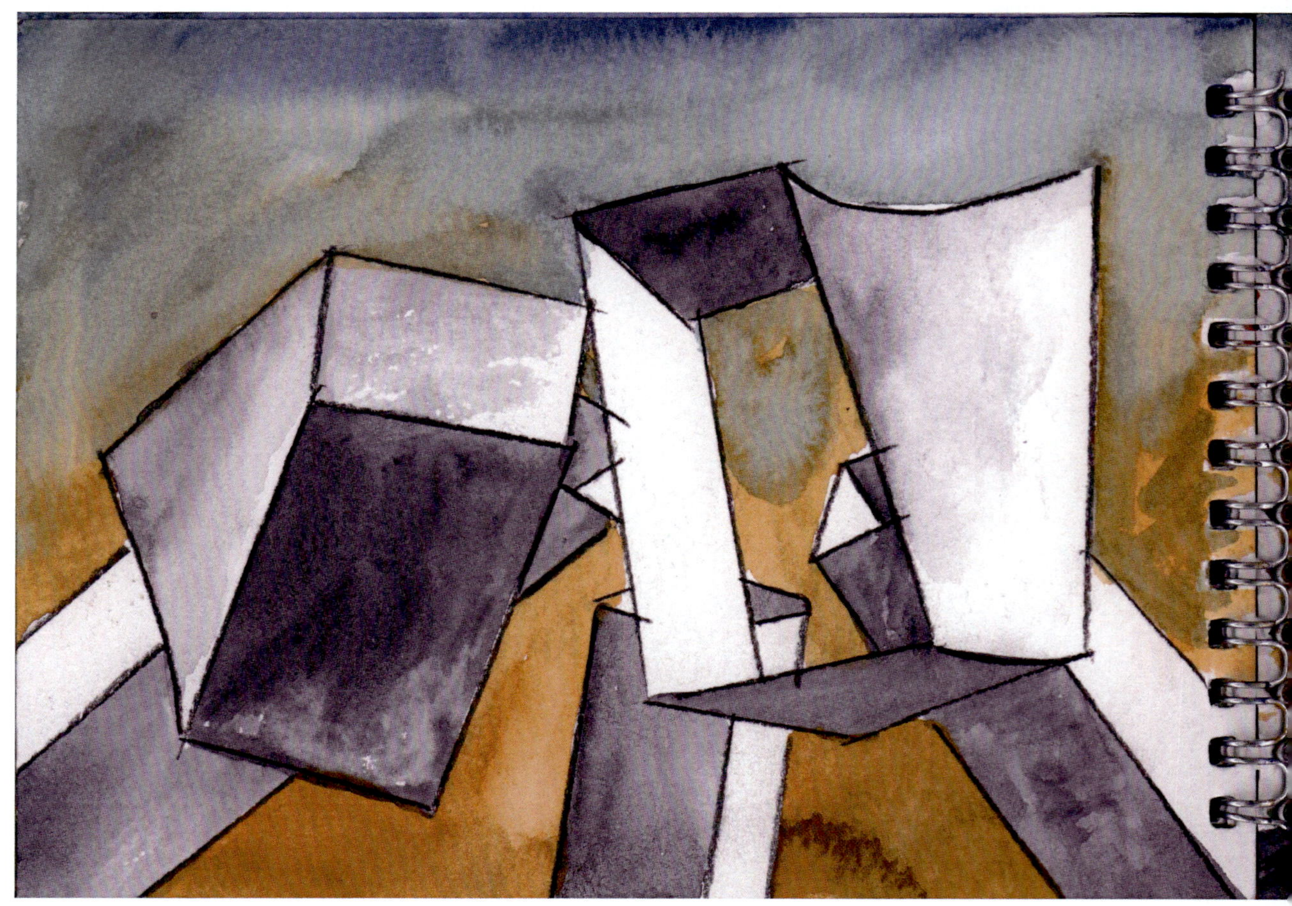

time," suggesting that there are many parallel times in the world of contemporary art. The building has four galleries, each with a different character, calling into question the notion of continuous time and the "grand narrative" of history.

The 41,000-square-foot building, with its inviting double-fronted forum opening to a serene sculpture garden, will provide spatial energy for important cutting-edge contemporary art exhibitions. Propelled by the university's top-ranked School of the Arts, the architecture becomes an instrument for exhibitions, film screenings, public lectures, performances, symposia, and community events engaging the university, the city, and beyond.

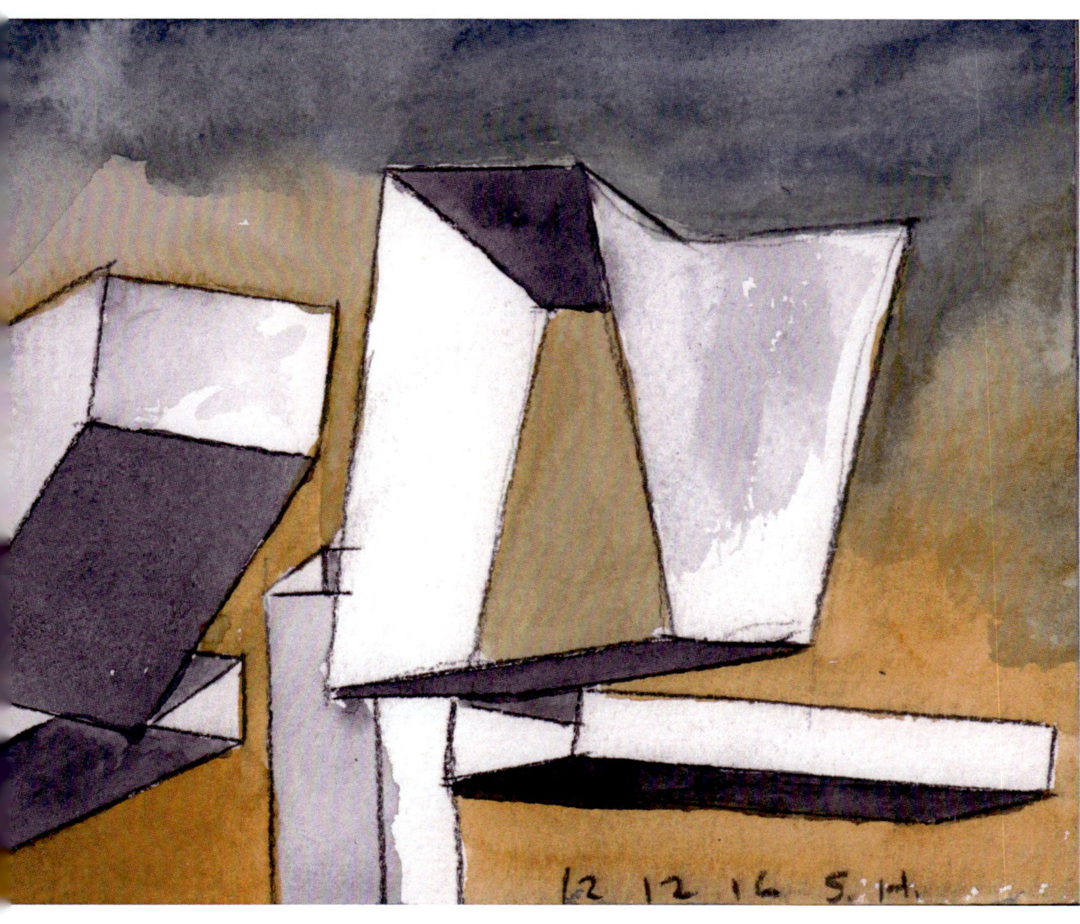

Steven Holl, *Abstraction for the Institute for Contemporary Art, Virginia Commonwealth University, Richmond, VA*, 2016, watercolor. Courtesy of Steven Holl.

MUSEUM OF FINE ARTS, HOUSTON
EXPANSION
Houston, Texas
2011–2019

The expansion of the Museum of Fine Arts unites its Fayez S. Sarofim campus and the community, with a new horizontal extension of landscape that will serve as a unifying character for the entire campus. The new 164,000-square-foot museum building is shaped by gardens of horizontal porosity that are open on all sides. In addition, a public plaza will be integrated with the new 80,000-square-foot Glassell School of Art.

Holl shaped this project according to five strategies:
CAMPUS: Integral experience
POROSITY: Seven porous gardens / social space
LIGHT: Luminous canopy
CIRCULATION: Gallery rooms and open flow
ARCHITECTURE: Complementary contrast

To realize a horizontal campus unity, all parking will be below ground. Visitors arriving by car will begin the museum experience in a lower arrival hall and sculpture court, directly connected to the new lobby and the Caroline Wiess Law Building.

The existing Lillie and Hugh Roy Cullen Sculpture Garden by Isamu Noguchi is horizontal and slow moving. The new Brown Foundation Plaza will be a zone of activity that will complement the spaces of contemplation and reflection, and continue the inspiring character of the new extension along Montrose Street. All the street edges of the museum building will be open and inviting, celebrating the unique qualities of an urban campus.

The new Glassell School of Art (2011–2018) is made of exposed planar structural pieces of sandblasted precast concrete. Beginning with the angle of the inclined plane that leads to the walkable roof garden, a series of similar angles are deployed in the precast planar planes yielding a rhythm of verticals and slight angles. These panels hold up the floors and reflect the scale of the school's studios on its exterior. Between the structural planes, special insulated translucent glass is mixed with clear glass providing great natural light to all studios and classrooms. All studios and classrooms have at least one operable widow. The building brackets the Brown Foundation Plaza and extends the campus landscape onto the roof culminating in a trellised roof garden. Horizontal activity, transparency and porosity will unify and integrate the new MFAH as an integrated campus experience. The lush Houston vegetation, refreshing sound, and reflections in water are all part of a new campus experience elevating the surprise and poetry of art

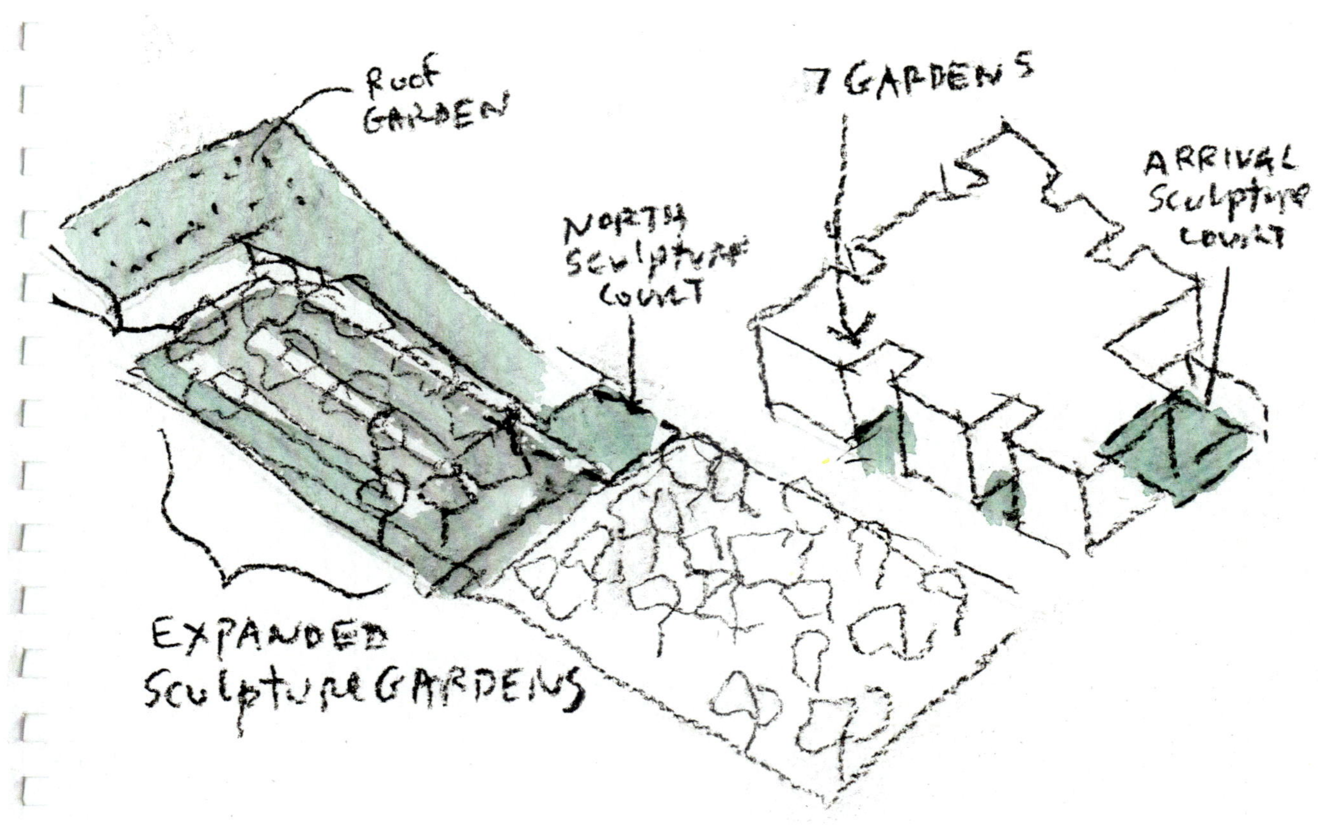

Steven Holl, *The campus extension of the Museum of Fine Arts; Houston*, 2012, watercolor on paper. Courtesy of Steven Holl.

THE JOHN F. KENNEDY CENTER FOR THE PERFORMING ARTS EXPANSION
Washington, District of Columbia
2012–2018

As a living memorial to John F. Kennedy, the 35th President of the United States, the Center for the Performing Arts takes an active position among the great presidential monuments dedicated to Thomas Jefferson and Abraham Lincoln in Washington, DC. Steven Holl and his team envision the expansion of the building as a fusion with the landscape and the adjacent Potomac River, rather than an appendage object within the landscape.

Steven Holl, *Drawing for the Planned JFK Center for the Performing Arts Expansion, 'Three white concrete pavilions: entry, glissando, river,' Washington, DC*, 2015, watercolor. Courtesy of Steven Holl.

In this project, Steven Holl has created an innovative design that preserves the silhouette of the current building while providing rehearsal rooms, classrooms, a lecture hall, multipurpose meeting rooms, and an event space. Located south of the existing facility, the expansion will feature interior spaces with soaring ceilings filled with natural light.

The open and engaging landscape will provide small and intimate spaces to gather and visit throughout the day. An exterior wall will be a home for broadcasts and simulcast performances from within the Kennedy Center and elsewhere. A restful grove of thirty-five ginkgo trees will acknowledge President Kennedy's position as the thirty-fifth president of the United States. An infinity pool will offer a direct sightline to Theodore Roosevelt Island across the Potomac River. The varied gardens will provide opportunities for casual performances and events, and other flexible locations will facilitate enhanced engagement, further positioning the center as a nexus of arts, learning, and culture in the years ahead.

The Kennedy Center's connection to the Potomac River will finally be achieved more than fifty years after it was lost in Edward Durell Stone's initial design, allowing easy access to and from the Rock Creek Trail and the Georgetown waterfront. The River Pavilion will provide a participatory, interactive space for small-scale performances, intimate concerts, poetry readings, and other experiences that are not easily accommodated within the existing building. The new addition will expand upon and improve the memorialization of President Kennedy and his significant contribution to the arts and American culture.

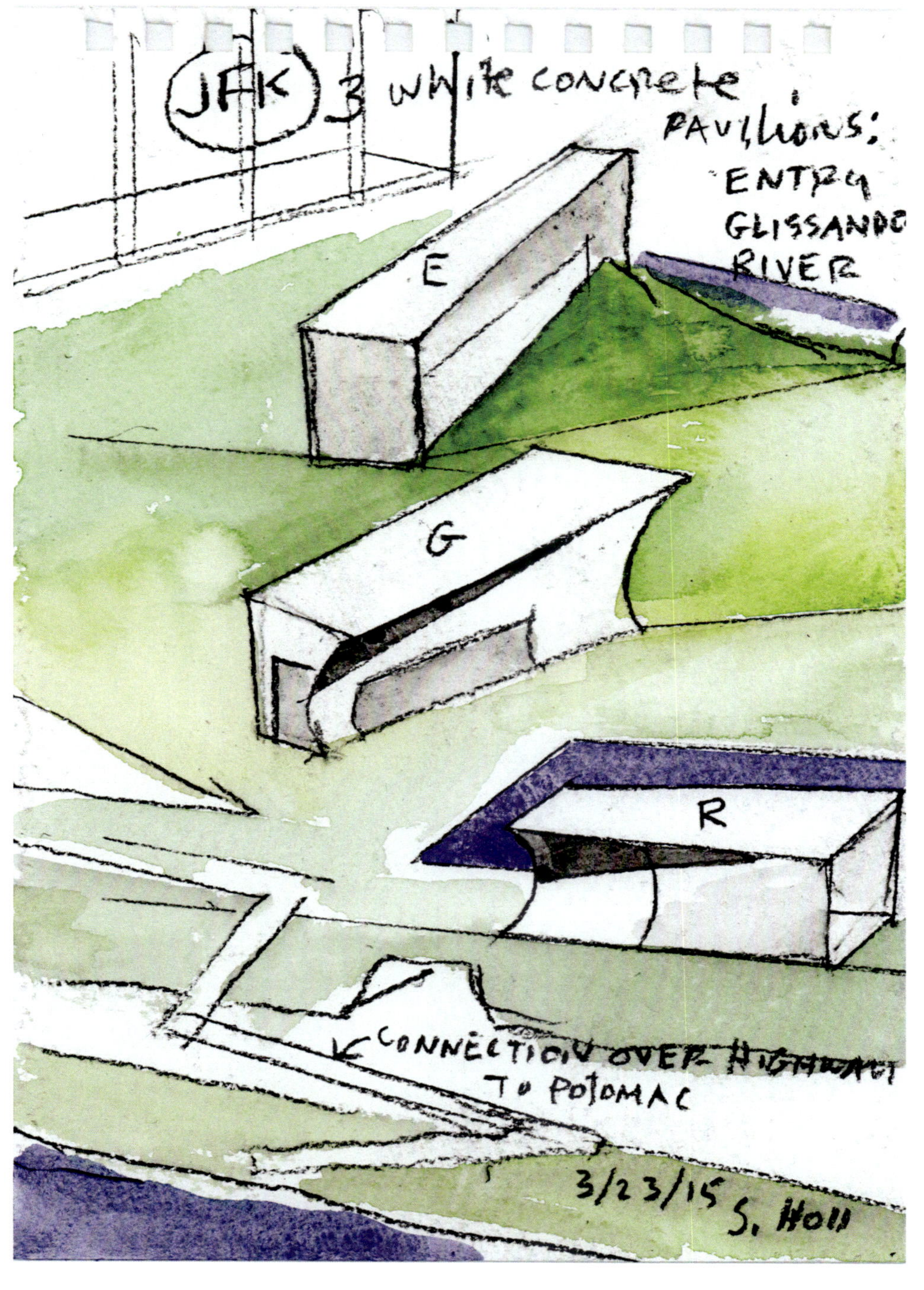
JFK
3 white concrete
PAVILIONS:
ENTRY
GLISSAND
RIVER
E
G
R
CONNECTION OVER HIGHWAY
TO POTOMAC
3/23/15
S. Holl

OCEANIC PAVILION

ChinPaiSan Necropolis, Taiwan
2013–2018

Located on a magnificent ocean-view site forty minutes from Taipei, the Necropolis of ChinPaoSan requires a new arrival hall to serve the complex, which has 10,000 existing burial sites, and a new pavilion for 150,000 additional ashbox locations. The arrival building will contain a 21-room hotel, a restaurant, a ceremonial chapel, an auditorium, and two small museums. The new pavilion will accommodate 1,000 people for ceremonial days, as well as fifty presiding Buddhist monks conducting ceremonies. An adjoining amphitheater offers seating for 5,000 people.

Through an exploration of more than thirty schemes in a search for a sacred space suitable for the site, watercolor drawings of

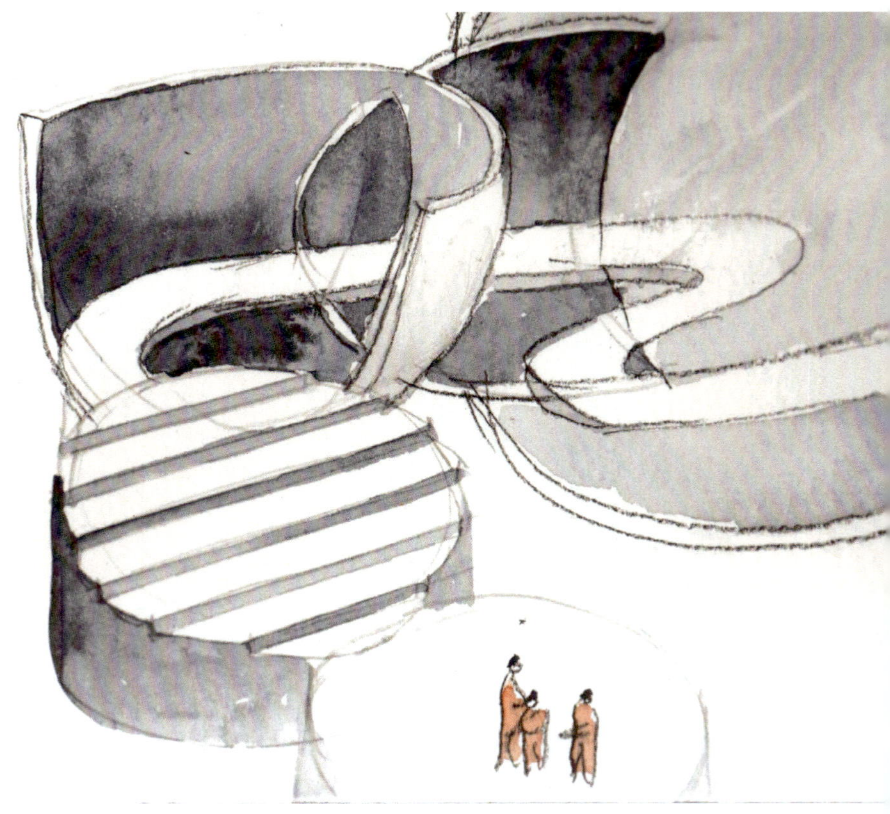

intersecting circles with their inherent universal properties and suggestive circulation typologies gradually became intersecting spheres. Model studies, which yielded amazing overlapping perspectives, created an astonishing spatial energy. The geometry of these intersected spheres refers back to a rich ancient history of symbolism: Borromean rings, which appear in Buddhist art, Viking rune stones, and Roman mosaics from thousands of years ago. Borromean rings represent the karmic laws of the universe and the interconnectedness of life. Christians have also used this symbol to represent the unity of the Holy Trinity. In the I Ching, the earth is represented as a square and the heavens as a circle. Here, the intersecting spheres are embedded in a rectangular plan topped by a sheet of water, pulling the ocean horizon into the composition.

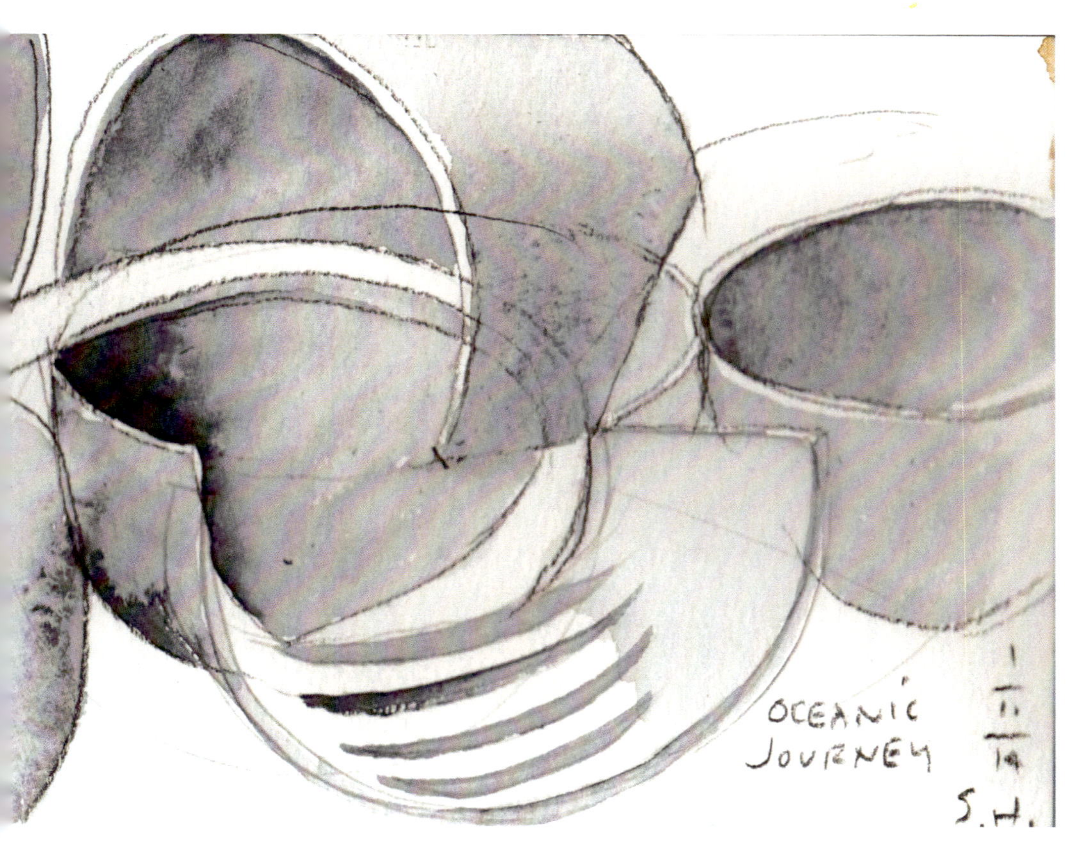

Steven Holl, *Study for "Oceanic Journey" for the Planned ChinPaoSan Necropolis, Taipei, Taiwan*, 2014, watercolor. Courtesy of Steven Holl.

Ex of IN HOUSE
Rhinebeck, New York
2015–2016

The Ex of IN House explores a language of space aimed at inner spatial energy that is strongly bound to the specific ecology of the place, while questioning current clichés of architectural language and commercial practice. The house is a built manifestation of the research and development project Explorations of IN, which has been in development at Steven Holl Architects since June 2014.

As a compact form measuring 918 square feet on a site of twenty-eight preserved rural acres, the house serves as an alternative to modernist suburban houses that "sprawl in the landscape." Instead, the Ex of IN is a house of compression and inner voids. The house's geometry is formed from spherical spaces intersecting with tesseract trapezoids intended as a catalyst of volumetric inner space. The geometry of the spherical intersections begins to be felt at the entry porch, where an orb of wood carved out of the house volume welcomes the entrant.

The shift in section of the house alters internal space with vertical dynamic spatial overlap. Situated around one main volume open to the second level, with the kitchen placed in the center, the house creates alternative use patterns. There are zero bedrooms, yet the house can sleep five.

Instead of using fossil fuel, the house is heated geothermally. Instead of grid power, the house has electricity from the sun.

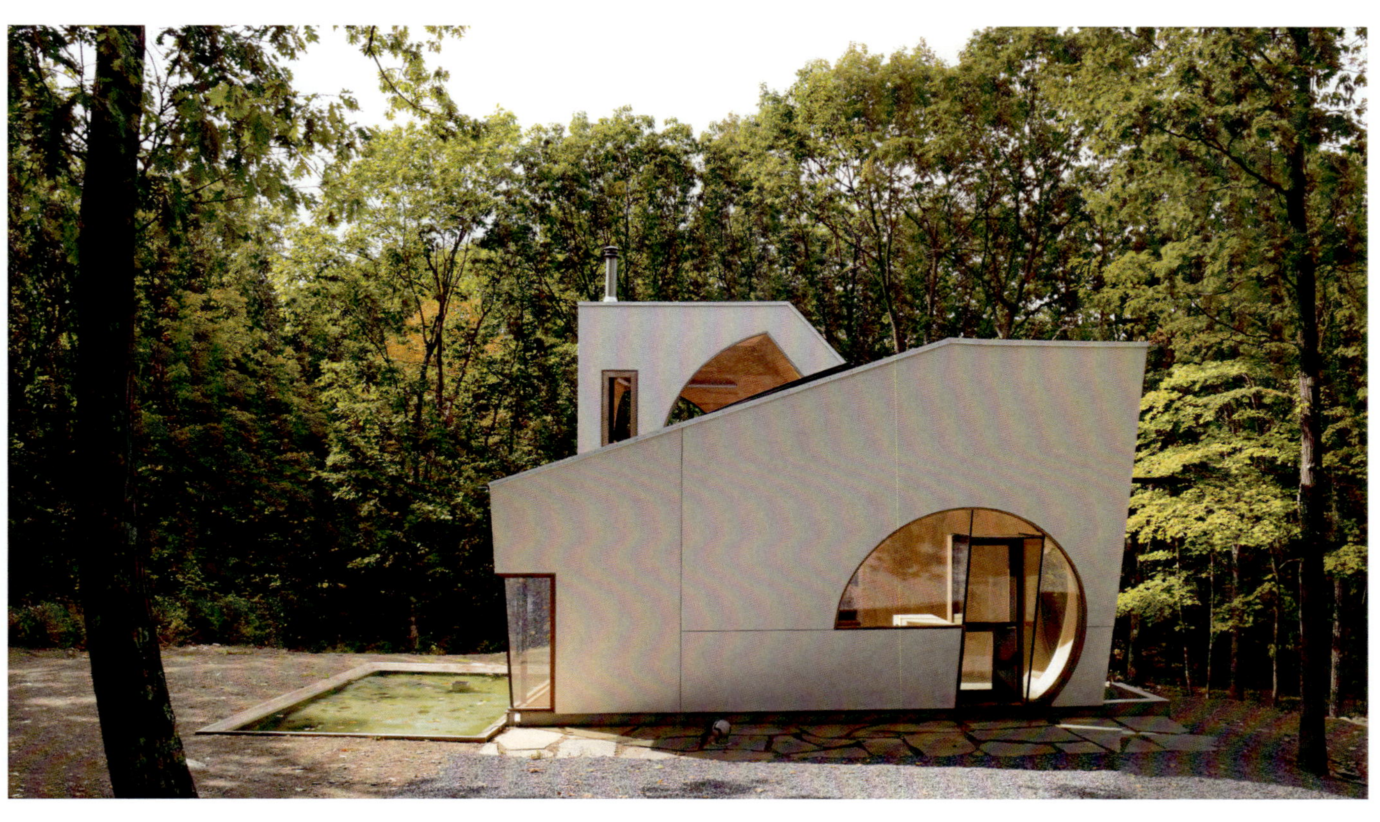

Steven Holl Architects,
Ex of IN House (exterior), 2017.
Photograph courtesy of
Paul Warchol.

RUBENSTEIN COMMONS
INSTITUTE FOR ADVANCED STUDIES
Princeton, New Jersey
2015–2018

The Institute for Advanced Study (IAS) in Princeton, established in 1930, is developing a new commons building on its historic campus near the original 1939 building, Fuld Hall, where Albert Einstein spent his last productive years.

The building weaves through the landscape, connecting with pools of water on the north, south, east, and west. The pools (which also contain underwater photovoltaics) reflect sunlight into interior spaces to produce an atmosphere of reflection. Here, natural phenomena are intertwined with science, physics, humanities, and art—corresponding with the institute's mission. Prismatic glass, located above seven feet, breaks white light into the color spectrum, to energize the interior with natural phenomena.

The landscape around the pools measures the span of a year through the four seasons. Near the east pool, pink-blooming magnolias signify spring. Summer is marked along the south pools with birch trees. The golden leaves of ginkgo trees on the west embody autumn, and pine trees representing winter occupy the moss gardens around the north pools. The geometry of the structure is formed by "space curves," where two non-planar curves intersect. The director of the IAS has remarked that the curved ceilings allow room for the "thought bubbles" of the scholars.

The Rubenstein Commons will support community and academic life on the IAS campus, promoting communication and collaboration through a variety of social and meeting spaces. In addition to providing a communal and flexible gathering place for the institute's research community, the building offers a space for the display of images and materials that tell the story of the institute's heritage, its extraordinary scholarly community, and its current and future efforts.

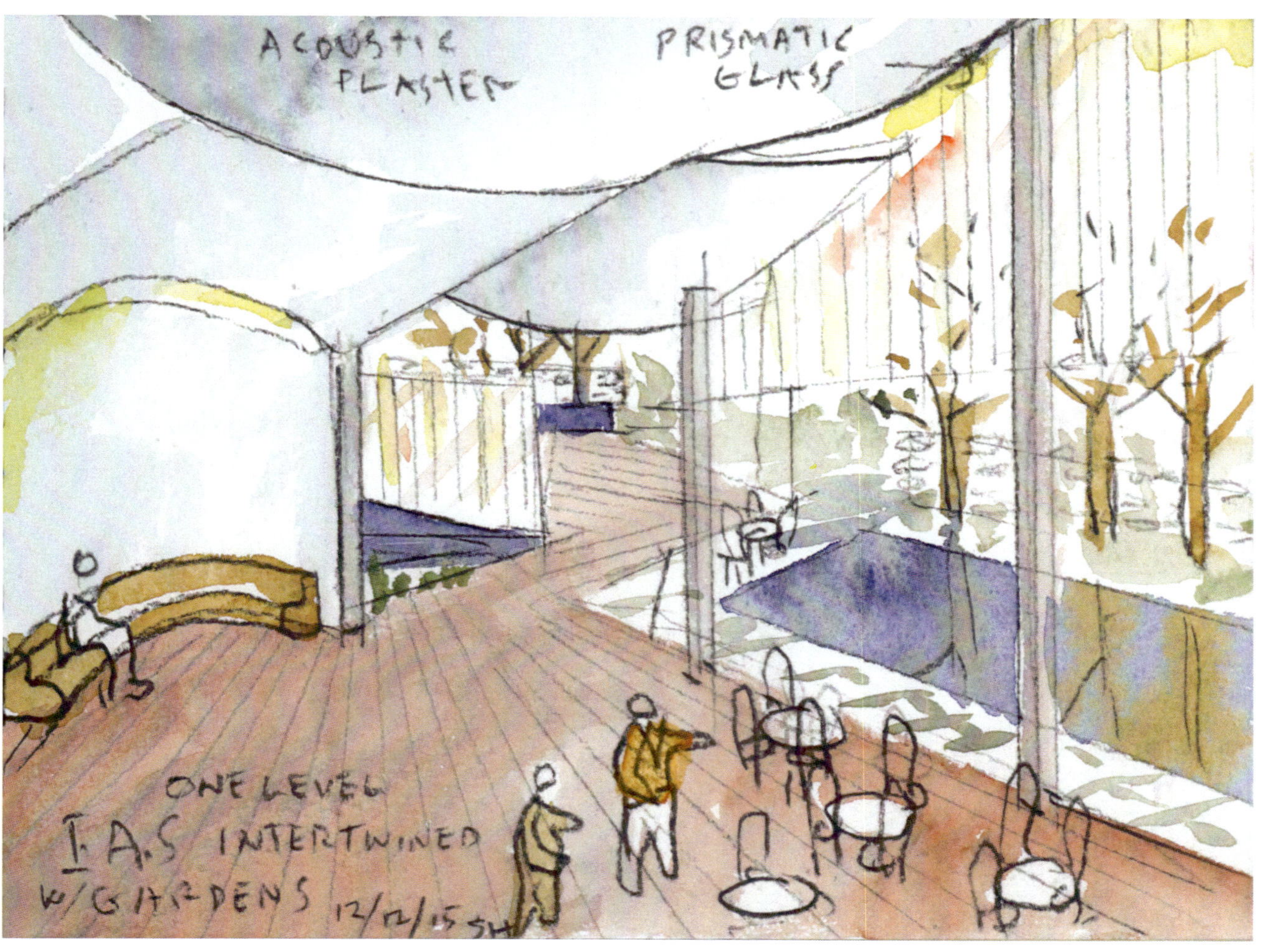

Steven Holl, *Study of the Planned Institute for Advanced Study, Billowing Commons Space Intertwined with Gardens, Princeton, NJ*, 2015, watercolor. Courtesy of Steven Holl.

FINE ARTS BUILDING
FRANKLIN & MARSHALL COLLEGE
Lancaster, Pennsylvania
2016–2019

On the historic campus of Franklin & Marshall College, a new fine arts building replaces the Herman Arts Center, built in 1969. Holl's building is the first phase of a proposed New Arts Quad that will define the southwest entrance to Franklin & Marshall's campus.

Large-diameter old-growth trees, the oldest elements of the campus, were the conceptual generator of the building's geometry. The raised pavilion takes its shape from the concave inflection of the trees, all of which are preserved on the site. A lightweight building, its main floor is lifted into the trees, with the ground level open to Buchanan Park and the Arts Quad.

The billowing, suspended, lightweight architecture of the new building is articulated with thin in-wall trusses, like those of a box kite. Like the heavy trunks of the nearby trees, the concrete walls at the ground level articulate the distinction between light and heavy. The skin is made of a new, recycled-glass aggregate material called Poraver, with natural light to all studios provided by Okalux insulated-channel glass and skylights. There are operable glass windows in every studio.

The state-of-the-art geothermal heating and cooling of the new building, and its super-insulated envelope, aspire to a future architecture of near net zero energy. A large reflecting pool doubles as campus stormwater overflow. At night, the reflections of the hovering building, glowing in the water, add to the special articulation of this place.

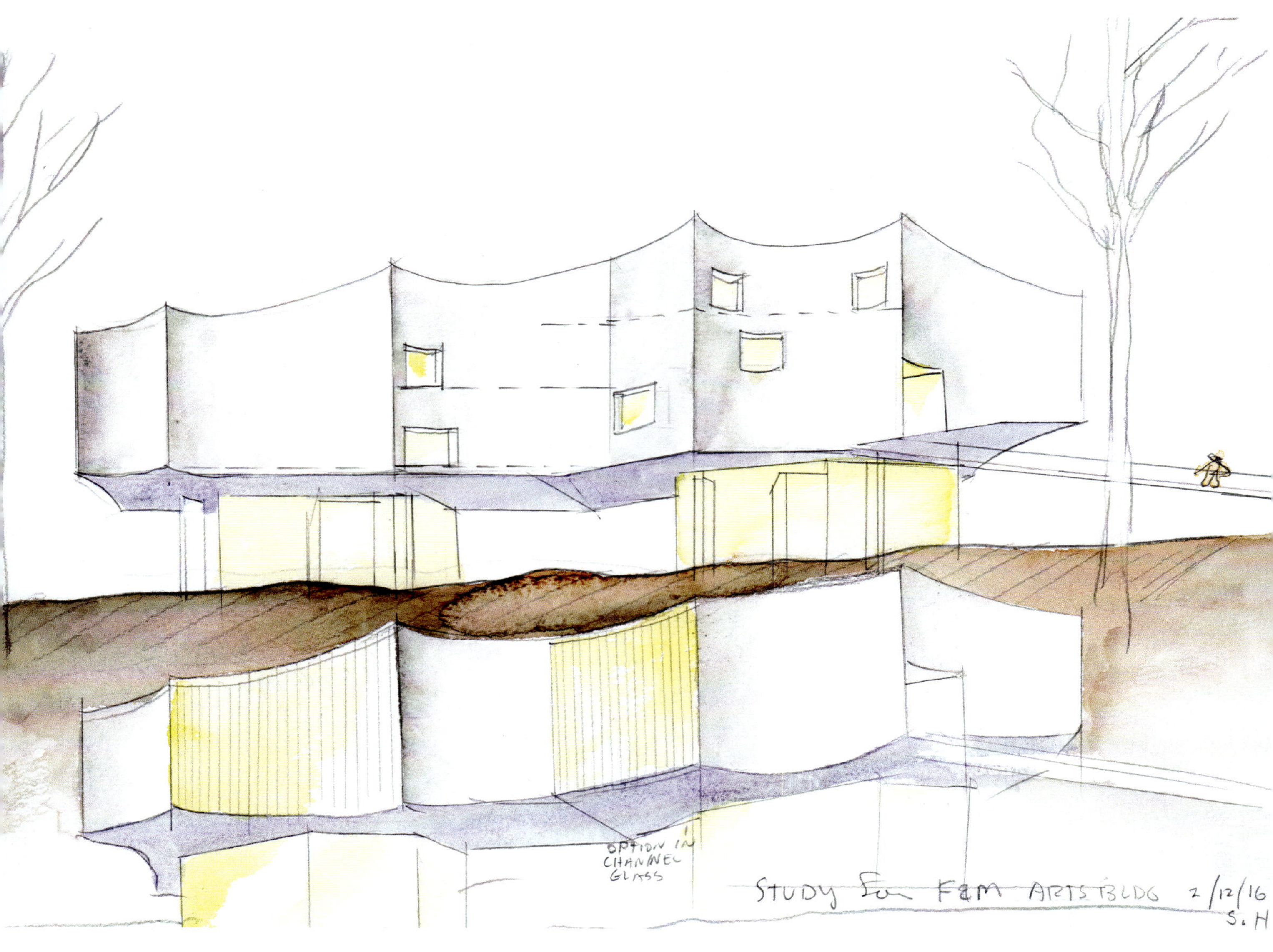

Steven Holl, *Study for F&M Arts Bldg*, Franklin & Marshall College, Lancaster, PA, 2016, watercolor. Courtesy of Steven Holl.

MALAWI LIBRARY
Lilongwe, Malawi
2017–2019

The 66,000-square-foot Malawi Library is organized around a section that provides maximum reflected light to the interior with optimum solar photovoltaic collection on the roofs. Natural light bouncing off curved, prefabricated roof structures made of Ductile concrete illuminates the space like a "field within a field." The free-plan library has meeting rooms and archives encased in glass for sound isolation and humidity control. A central rain-collecting pool demarcates the main circulation desk and reflects cloud-like light that ripples through the roof geometry like a wave field.

The library's construction will utilize local materials and local labor. Screens of locally crafted bamboo plywood define the building perimeter, offering a shaded arcade space surrounding the building. The comfort concept is based on the local identity of the site, which has an altitude of 1,250 meters, with high solar gains from its sun positions, a temperature profile dominated by the rainy season with a few peaks above 35°C, and cool nights below 22°C.

An ambitious cross-ventilation system enables optimum temperature control without any mechanical conditioning, with the curved roof blades allowing load-free daylight supply from the south to maximize the energy-collection surfaces.

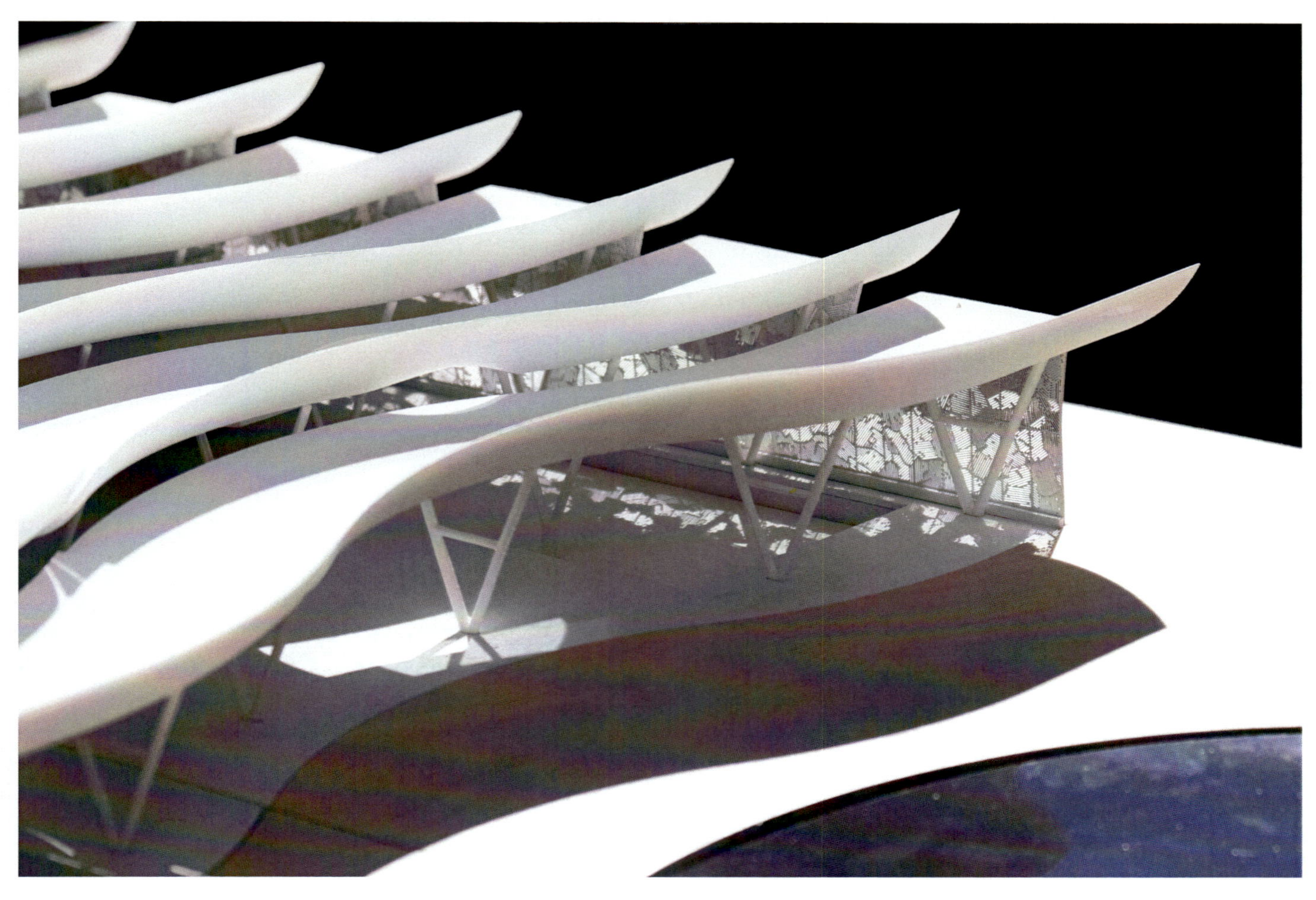

Steven Holl Architects,
Model, Malawi Library (detail),
Lilongwe, Malawi, 2017.
Courtesy Steven Holl Architects.

EXHIBITION CHECKLIST

ALL WORKS BY STEVEN HOLL AND COURTESY OF STEVEN HOLL ARCHITECTS UNLESS OTHERWISE NOTED

Study for Porous School of Music, 10/14/2007, 2007
Pigment print on watercolor paper
5 × 7 in.

Architecture = Music, 10/15/2007, 2007
Pigment print on watercolor paper
5 × 7 in.

3 Buildings Joined, 10/15/2007, 2007
Pigment print on watercolor paper
16 × 13 in.

3 Buildings, One Collective Space, 10/26/2007, 2007
Pigment print on watercolor paper
16 × 13 in.

Acoustic Suspended Practice Rooms, 11/16/2007, 2007
Pigment print on watercolor paper
5 × 7 in.

Black Box to the White Cube, 11/17/2007, 2007
Pigment print on watercolor paper
5 × 14 in.

Dancing Stair, 02/17/2012, 2012
Pigment print on watercolor paper
20 × 12 in.

Suprematism of Mind, 11/22/2007, 2007
Pigment print on watercolor paper
5 × 7 in.

Digitally-Cut Lecce Stone, 07/20/2010, 2010
Pigment print on watercolor paper
10 × 7 in.

Proportions Fibonacci, 01/06/2012, 2012
Pigment print on watercolor paper
5 × 7 in.

Individual and Collective 1, 01/06/2012, 2012
Pigment print on watercolor paper
5 × 7 in.

Individual and Collective 2, 01/06/2012, 2012
Pigment print on watercolor paper
5 × 7 in.

Dance Poetry and Music, 01/29/2012, 2012
Pigment print on watercolor paper
10 × 7 in.

Elevations and Entry Level Plan, 09/12/2010, 2010
Pigment print on watercolor paper
10 × 8 in.

Looking Up from Entry, 08/23/2010, 2010
Pigment print on watercolor paper
5 × 7 in.

Great Public Activity Spaces, 08/13/2010, 2010
Pigment print on watercolor paper
5 × 7 in.

Queens West Library, 09/13/2010, 2010
Pigment print on watercolor paper
5 × 7 in.

A Series of Change in Space, 09/01/2010, 2010
Pigment print on watercolor paper
5 × 7 in.

Children's Library, 09/12/2010, 2010
Pigment print on watercolor paper
5 × 7 in.

Manhattan View, 05/19/2010, 2010
Pigment print on watercolor paper
8 1/2 × 11 in.

Galleries in Forking Time, 10/06/2011, 2011
Pigment print on watercolor paper
5 × 7 in.

Abstraction, 12/12/2016, 2016
Pigment print on watercolor paper
5 × 14 in.

Forum, 09/12/2011, 2011
Pigment print on watercolor paper
9 × 12 in.

7 Porous Gardens, January 2012, 2012
Pigment print on watercolor paper
9 3/4 × 7 in.

Luminous Canopy, January 2012, 2012
Pigment print on watercolor paper
5 × 7 in.

Spatial Flow through Natural Light, 10/03/2011, 2011
Pigment print on watercolor paper
5 × 7 in.

5 Lines from the Hand & Notes of Colored Glass, 01/21/2012, 2012
Pigment print on watercolor paper
5 × 14 in.

Neume Notation, 01/23/2012, 2012
Watercolor on paper
5 × 7 in.

Potomac Pavilions, 06/22/2012, 2012
Watercolor on paper
5 × 7 in.

Kennedy Center Extensions, 07/08/2012, 2012
Pigment print on watercolor paper
5 × 14 in.

3 White Concrete Pavilions, 03/23/2015, 2015
Pigment print on watercolor paper
5 × 7 in.

3 Half Domes Face Ocean Horizon, 12/16/2013, 2013
Pigment print on watercolor paper
5 × 14 in.

Arrival Hall, 12/12/2013, 2013
Pigment print on watercolor paper
5 × 7 in.

Between Being and Non-Being, 12/08/2013, 2013
Pigment print on watercolor paper
5 × 14 in.

Oceanic Journey, 01/11/2014, 2014
Pigment print on watercolor paper
5 × 14 in.

Space Curve, 06/04/2016, 2016
Pigment print on watercolor paper
5 × 7 in.

Intertwining Enmeshing, 11/09/2015, 2015
Pigment print on watercolor paper
5 × 7 in.

Space Curves, 06/14/2016, 2016
Pigment print on watercolor paper
5 × 7 in.

Space Merged with Natural Phenomena, 11/09/2015, 2015
Pigment print on watercolor paper
10 × 7 in.

Study for F&M Arts Building, 02/12/2016, 2016
Pigment print on watercolor paper
10 × 7 in.

F&M Arts Quad, 02/11/2016, 2016
Pigment print on watercolor paper
10 × 7 in.

Studio for Arts, 01/31/2016, 2016
Pigment print on watercolor paper
5 × 7 in.

Study, 05/16/2016, 2016
Pigment print on watercolor paper
5 × 7 in.

Malawi Campus Study, 10/02/2016, 2016
Pigment print on watercolor paper
10 × 7 in.

Open-Air Library, 10/03/2016, 2016
Watercolor on paper
5 × 7 in.

EX of IN (Chapel), 02/17/2015, 2015
Pigment print on watercolor paper
5 × 7 in.

The White—the Black & Spherical Intersections, 02/27/2015, 2015
Pigment print on watercolor paper
5 × 14 in.

Study, 07/05/2015, 2015
Pigment print on watercolor paper
5 × 14 in.

South = White / East = Yellow, 03/14/2015, 2015
Pigment print on watercolor paper
5 × 14 in.

Study, 04/04/2015, 2015
Pigment print on watercolor paper
5 × 7 in.

Door Handle, 2014
Cast silicone bronze
8 × 8 × 4 in.

Door Handle, 2014
Cast silicone bronze
8 × 8 × 4 in.

Formwork, for Crinkle Concrete Mock-Up, June 2015, 2015
Cast rubber on wrinkled aluminum
23 × 22 × 2 1/2 in.

Wall-Sconce, 2016
3D-printed, cornstarch-based bioplastic
12 × 8 × 8 in.

5 Small Exploration Models and Tracing Paper (4 Intersecting Spheres 07/07/2014, Inversion 08/07/2014, Tesseract Fragments 08/29/2014, Insertion Inversion 08/30/2014, Ex of IN House Feb. 2015), 2014–15
Resin-impregnated plaster 3D print
6 × 6 × 6 in. each

Door Handle, 2015
Cast silicone bronze
14 × 8 × 8 in.

Princeton Wall-Sconce Mock-Up Short Version, 2015
CNC-milled solid walnut and LED Light
42 × 6 × 6 in.

Early Concept Study Model, 2007
Chipboard and acrylic
13 × 12 in.

Early Concept Study Model, 2007
Painted plywood, wood blocks, cork, and acrylic
14 × 14 × 7 in.

Competition Study Model, December 2015, 2015
Resin-impregnated plaster 3D print, copper patina paint
8 × 8 × 4 in.

Final Scheme Competition Model, November 2015, 2015
Resin-impregnated plaster 3D print
8 × 8 × 4 in.

Construction Documents Facade Model, 2017
Acrylic tubes and chipboard
4 × 12 1/2 × 30 in.

Early Concept Model Submitted for Competition, Early 2012, 2012
CNC-milled acrylic, sanded
12 1/2 × 9 1/2 × 2 in.

Early Concept Study Model, Late 2014, 2014
Resin-impregnated plaster 3D print
8 × 6 × 4 in.

Study Model VCU, 2012
Resin-impregnated plaster 3D print, silver paint
8 × 8 × 5 in.

100% Schematic Design Presentation Model, April 2012, 2012
Resin-impregnated plaster 3D print, silver paint
23 × 43 × 18 in.

Ex of IN XII, 2015
CNC-milled walnut
25 × 30 × 23 1/2 in.
Fabricated by Wala-Wala Founding

Schematic Design Study Model, mid-2013, 2013
Resin-impregnated plaster 3D prints on chipboard, acrylic base
58 × 41 × 15 in.

Concept Model, 2013
Cast concrete and plywood
41 × 44 × 16 in.

Sectional Study Model, End of Design Development, Late 2012, 2012
Museum board, plywood, laser-cut paper, and cork, silver paint
31 1/2 × 10 × 21 in., scale: 1:48

First Conceptual Site Model, 2010
Painted museum board and acrylic
24 × 24 in., scale: 3:32

50% Design Development Presentation Model, 2017
Resin-impregnated plaster 3D print and laser-cut paper, white paint, CNC-milled plywood, and acrylic base
44 × 33 × 8 in., scale 1:100

Final Presentation Model, May 2015, 2015
Resin-impregnated plaster 3D print, painted, sanded acrylic, and steel wool on CNC-milled plywood base
49 × 29 × 13 in.

Study Model, 2015
Resin-impregnated plaster 3D print, plywood, and acrylic
25 × 17 × 18 in.

Buddha Hall and Tree of Life Interior Study Model, 2017
Resin-impregnated plaster 3D print, white paint, plywood, and acrylic
18 × 36 × 27 1/2 in., scale 1:50

Study Model for Arrival Hall and Light Monitors, 2017
Resin-impregnated plaster 3D print, colored acrylic
33 × 12 × 17 in., scale 1:50

50% Design Development Presentation Model, Late 2016, 2016
Resin-impregnated plaster 3D print and acrylic on chipboard base
36 × 46 × 25 in., scale: 1:64

100% Design Development Sectional Presentation Model, February 2017, 2017
Resin-impregnated plaster 3D print, copper patina paint
20 × 52 × 10 in.

Spirit of Space
Maggie's Centre Barts, London, 2013
Film (color, sound)
6 min., 51 sec.

Spirit of Space
Ex of IN House, 2017
Film (color, sound)
6 min., 30 sec.

Spirit of Space
Dance with Architecture (Jessica Lang & Steven Holl), 2016
Film (color, sound)
12 min., 15 sec.

Spirit of Space
Institute for Contemporary Art, VCU, 2014
Film (color, sound)
5 min., 46 sec.

Spirit of Space
Sifang Art Museum: A Conversation with Steven Holl, 2014
Film (color, sound)
5 min., 19 sec.

Spirit of Space
INVERSION—Milan, 2013
Film (color, sound)
2 min., 54 sec.

Spirit of Space
Daeyang Gallery and House: A Conversation with Steven Holl, 2012
Film (color, sound)
4 min., 43 sec.

Custom rug for Lewis Center for the Arts, 2017
Cotton weave with Himalayan wool pile
6 × 7 ft.
Fabricated by cc Tapis, made in Nepal

Custom rug for Ex of IN House, 2017
Wool
6 × 9 ft.
Fabricated by cc Tapis, made in Nepal

Published on the occasion of the exhibition *Steven Holl: Making Architecture*, curated by Nina Stritzler-Levine, on view from February 10 to July 15, 2018, in the Morgan Anderson Gallery and Howard Greenberg Gallery at the Samuel Dorsky Museum of Art, State University of New York at New Paltz. The exhibition is also on view as follows: October 1–28, 2018, Soongsil University Gallery, Seoul, Korea; and November 9, 2018–January 11, 2019, Seoul City Museum, Seoul, Korea.

Support for the Dorsky Museum's exhibitions and programs is provided by Friends of the Samuel Dorsky Museum of Art and the State University of New York at New Paltz.

Steven Holl: Making Architecture
Published by the Samuel Dorsky Museum of Art
State University of New York at New Paltz
One Hawk Drive
New Paltz, NY

Designed by Jeff Lesperance
Edited by Kristin Swan
Copyedited by Amy Pickering
Printed by Bookmobile
This book is typeset in Berthold Akzidenz Grotesk. It is printed on 80lb. matte text and 120lb matte cover.
Distributed by the State University of New York Press (www.sunypress.edu)

ISBN: 978-0-9982075-6-8

Collaborators for the realization of all projects presented by Steven Holl Architects include:
Partners: Chris McVoy, Noah Yaffe and Roberto Bannura
Directors: Molly Blieden, Eleanore Ho
Associates: Olaf Schmidt, JongSeo Lee, Garrick Ambrose, Marcus Carter, Filipe Taboada, Dimitra Tsachrelia, Christina Yessios
Project Architects: Wenying Sun, Yiqing Zhao, Peter Chang, Suk Lee, Carolina Cohen Freue, Magdalena I. Naydekova, Ruoyu Wei, and Whitney Forward
Team: Lourenzo Amaro de Oliveira, Seo Hee Lee, Zhu Zhu, Tsung-Yen Hsieh, Yuanchu Yi
Fabrication: Michael Haddy
Staff: Sarah Coote, Julie Heffernan, Alessandra Catherine Calaguire
Press: Julia van der Hout, Camille Newton

Back Cover: *Study on the concept of "World/House" for the Ex of IN House* (detail), Rhinebeck, New York, 2015, Watercolor. Courtesy of Steven Holl.

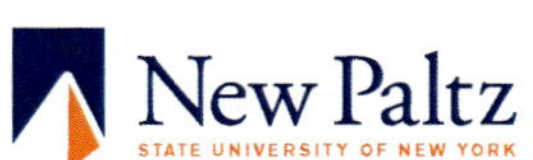

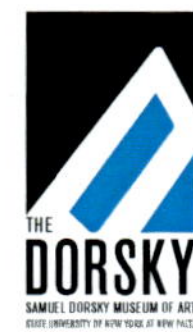